DARING TO GO BEYOND YOUR DREAMS

DARING TO GO BEYOND YOUR DREAMS

"...ALL THINGS ARE POSSIBLE TO HIM THAT BELIEVES."

DENNIS DRAKE

ED&C PUBLISHING

A Department of Excel Development & Communications (ED&C)

Manassas, Virginia

ED&C PUBLISHING 2000

Cover/Book design by Judi Lynn Lake
Edited by Shellie Hurrle

LIBRARY OF CONGRESS CATALOGING-IN-PUBLICATION DATA
Daring to Go Beyond Your Dreams/Dennis Drake

Library of Congress Control Number: 00-091118

ISBN 0-9700294-3-8

Printed in the United States of America

Lives of Great men all remind us
We can make our lives sublime,
And, departing, leave behind us
Footprints on the sands of time.

Footprints, that perhaps another,
Sailing o'er life's solemn main,
A forlorn and shipwrecked brother,
Seeing, shall take heart again.

Let us, then, be up and doing,
With a heart for any fate;
Still achieving, still pursuing,
Learn to labour and to wait.

—A Psalm of Life, 1839
Henry Wadsworth Longfellow

TABLE OF CONTENTS

ACKNOWLEDGMENTS

ALLOW ME TO say a word of thanks to my lovely mother, Leatrice Gerald, whose prayers kept me; whose can-do spirit, never-give-up attitude and total belief in me has been the North star of my life. Thanks to my grandmother, the late Lair Ruth Drake, whose love and support always made me believe in myself—that I, too, was someone special. I'd also like to thank the following: my youngest Sister, Tessa Gerald, for her individuality and strength to always be herself; my middle sister, Dolicia Gerald Kimbrough, for her kindness and gentle ways; my oldest sister, Delores Gerald, for her strength; my additional sister, Lisa Pickett, for her encouragement; my in-laws, Terry and Marie Armstrong, for their acceptance; my aunts and uncles and their families: Rufus, Charlie and Betty, George and Dorothy, Larry and Naomi, Ronald, Danny and Wanda, William Howard and Eleanor, Thelma, Brenda, and Betty and Michael; and the late Willie James, whose love, care, and encouragement in my youth has helped mold me into who I am today. Thanks to my godmother, Geneva, for her encouragement; Ella Mae and Dawn for their love; Kenny and Terrance Gerald for great childhood memories, Andrea Drake for your friendship when needed the most; the entire Drake, Patterson, and Gerald Families; Ernestine Rutherford, Robin Rutherford, and Sharon Bradford for their support; Cleveland and Leslie Davis, friends that help bring out the best in me; Shirley Thomas, my mom away from Mom; and my dear friend, Sabrina Bartley, whose belief in me gave me encouragement. Thanks to my dear friend, Shelia Hines, for her support and strength in helping me move beyond what I was. I would like to mention Eric and Cherita Allsbrook and Sonya and Tony Thomas, friends who will always be there; Joy Stevens for her beautiful spirit and understanding heart; Joe and Jackie Stevens, our other parents, for their example, encouragement and support; Anita Bradley for her support and honesty; Kedrick Screen, Jimmy Desantis and Leonard Screen, friends through it all; Diane Brooks for her encouragement; and Kenny and Manning Sarfin at Equitable Camera and Card Shop for giving me a chance and standing with me during difficult times. Thanks to the late Dr. Sandy F. Ray, Dr. Harry S. Wright, Reverend Henry G. Scott and the Cornerstone Baptist Church Family of Brooklyn New York for their wonderful teachings. I am grateful to Pastor Frederick Haynes of Friendship West Baptist Church (Dallas, Texas) for his wonderful example and to Reverend Robert Thomas, a friend and mentor in the faith. Special thanks to the following pastors and their congregation for their support and love: Pastor William Scott and the Divine Life family of Culppper, Virginia; Pastor Cherry and the Word Alive family of Manassas, Virginia; Pastor Lane and the Lord's Full Gospel Baptist Church family of Alexandria, Virginia; Pastor Brown and the Mount Zion family of Stafford, Virginia; Pastor Beandor and the Church on the Rock family of Dale City, Virginia; and to Pastor Ausbery and my church family at Antioch Baptist Church of Burke, Virginia. Special thanks to my Editor Shellie Hurrle and to my Graphic/Book Designer Judi Lynn Lake. Special thanks to my beautiful wife, Renita, for letting me write this book and motivating me to "Dare to Go Beyond My Dreams." Thank you for your love, which has taught me love, and your inspiring words that move my heart to action. I am grateful for the patience of my wonderful children, Dennis, Shayna, Devon, Elexus, and Ashton James Drake—our new edition to the family. Thank you to so many others, without whose encouragement and love, none of this could have been possible.

INTRODUCTION

IN HIS LAST days, my father said to me:

Dennis, don't feel sorry for me. I have lived my life, I have enjoyed my life, and I've done all that I wanted to do in life. I now know what it feels like to be Job. If God decides that it is time for me to die, I am ready. You go on and make the best of your life; don't waste time—you may just run out of it. Take advantage of every moment that God gives you, with everything that he has given you, and live your life today.

I have lived my life, I now know what it feels like to be Job, and don't waste time. These particular words remain with me, and I use them as motivation and inspiration. It is important to note that when my father said, "I have lived my life," I believe that he was referring to today's pursuit of money or material things being more important than happiness; these days we find ourselves making a living, yet not living our lives.

The second point, which will not be tackled in this book, but is worth mentioning: "I now know what it feels like to be Job." While it's true my father suffered a great deal in his last days, I feel he was actually talking about being worthy of God's tests in life.

The last point was that I should waste no time and take advantage of each day that God has given me. It is important to understand that each day is precious, and we should pay close attention and take advantage of the opportunities a day brings. We should do something each day to bring us closer to our full potential. This point is the main basis for this book.

One of the greatest tragedies in life is to go through each day without ever dreaming of what you can be, without a sense of purpose or hope for tomorrow. Somewhere along the way, many of us have somehow been robbed of our ability to dream or the strength to reach for our dreams. The thief can come in many forms: Poverty, self-doubt, low self-esteem, the pain and agony of facing defeat, and many other negative circumstances and situations in life can appear to rob us of our dreams. However, the thief can only take away our dreams, hopes, and purpose if we allow them to be taken. If complacency, fear, or unknown situations in life cause us to forfeit our dreams, we may never truly understand what it means to be us. We will go through life without the answer to the age-old question: Why are we here? Furthermore, we will never understand our purpose in life or reach our full potential.

Even more devastating than having no dreams is to have a dream and never do anything about it. It is tragic to have a fulfilling dream, something you know you can and should do, but lack the courage and commitment to make that dream a reality. I strongly believe that the actual act of working toward fulfillment of our dreams helps us identify our purpose in life. It is that dream that allows us to see who we really are and how truly wonderful it is to be ourselves.

So many have already made the inevitable march to the grave and have taken with them their dreams, depriving the world of their special offerings. In the final resting places of the world, we will find the other Bill Gateses, Reverend Dr. Martin Luther Kings, Anita Bakers, Maya Angelous, John F. Kennedys, Michael Jordans, James Geralds, and many others who went unnoticed. Why? Because they never dared to go beyond their dreams to make them a reality. Then there are, Unfortunately, the words of deep regrets that are common in those that have been here for quite some time and now are mature in age: *If only I would have . . . I should have done . . . I could have been . . . .* Those are just a few of the words from people that looked back on their lives and realized that they did not live up to their full potential and purpose. Those that have passed on with unfulfilled lives and the "If only I . . ." regrets of those that wished that they had done more should provide our motivation for pressing forward, to reach that mark toward which we are called.

One thing, before we go any further, I cannot emphasize enough: It is just as, if not more important to be working toward our dreams than it is to have actually achieved them. My father was completely happy doing what he did, not because he had obtained or achieved all that he wanted in life, but because he was living his dreams by working toward them.

In Philippians 3:12, 13, Paul says, "Not that I have already obtained all this, or have already been made perfect, but I press on to take hold of that which Christ Jesus took hold of me...." His words show us that we may not reach our mark, but it is important to know that we can live our lives and discover our purpose by working toward our dreams. It is the joy of the journey, more than the destination itself, which gives us fulfillment, focus, and purpose.

Moses's dream, his desire, was to guide his people into the Promised Land, but his actual purpose and fulfillment came while pressing to reach the Promised Land. Although he never made it, he lived out his purpose and his life had meaning through his forward movements.

Dr. Martin Luther King Jr. had great dreams of a time where there would be harmony among all races, creed, and colors. Although he did not live to see that day, his purpose in life was known and the fulfillment of his life was realized as he moved toward his dreams.

Thus, our dreams give us our purpose in life. By working toward those dreams, our lives take on meaning, fulfillment, and focus. Whether we reach our dreams or not, growth, fulfillment, happiness, and reward come during the journey itself. The experiences we gain while working toward our dreams provide the necessary equipment for achieving and living the dream.

Congratulations! Reading this book is the first of many steps in realizing your dream, not just thinking about it. By looking at where we came from, where we are, and where we want to go, we will use the inspiration that feeds our motivation and be the wonderful creatures we were designed to be. You will notice, while reading this book, that I repeat several topics and key points over and over again. That is because, I feel strongly that those points should be given extra special attention. Your time is precious, and I promise not to waste it while we explore life experiences, stories, and poems that reflect what it really means to be us.

I believe the Bible contains the greatest story ever told about going beyond our dreams. The magnificent story of Joseph, as told in Chapters 37-47 of Genesis, serves as my inspirational spark and was the primary motivation for writing this book. I pray that my sharing it will motivate and inspire you to achieve your dreams.

Young Joseph had a dream. He shared his dream with others, endured persecution as a result, turned his persecution into positive experiences, held on to his dreams, lived his dreams, and inevitably made his dreams a reality. Ultimately, after achieving his dream, Joseph discovered that the trials he'd endured had equipped him for handling any future situations. Working toward his dream gave his life meaning and fulfillment and became his true purpose in life. In itself, Joseph's dream was important, but so was Joseph's courage to go after it, the persistence to hold on to it, and the attitude and self-control to make it a reality.

As Joseph ultimately realized, we are meant to share our God-given dreams with the world. God has given all of us a special gift. God may not have given all of us everything, but He did give us all something—our dream—to offer hope, fulfillment, and purpose in our lives.

I frequently refer to the story of Joseph throughout this book, because it is not just another rags to riches story. It is a story about purpose, attitude, and positive responses that transform each setback into a step up. Rather than ask "Why?" during those setbacks, we learn to ask instead, "What shall our next step be?" The story proves how the reality of our dream is shaped by our mentality. In essence, the story dares us to go beyond our dreams to make them reality.

Time continues marching on, and you, too, can find yourself meeting your inevitable fate, that thing called death, with your dreams still within you—never to be seen, touched, or felt by those around you. You may someday say, like countless others, those words of deep regret, "If only I . . ." Time ticks on with or without you, and what you do today matters, because it will reflect upon your life tomorrow. Your actions today will determine what is said of you between your date of birth and date of death.

I believe you have already taken a very important step in achieving your dreams. You have announced, by purchasing this book, that you do have a dream, a purpose in life, and that you are ready to work toward the reality of your dreams and a fulfilled life. I pray that this book will be one of many catalysts that will motivate and inspire you to be all that you are and all that you were created to be. Please do not read this book expecting to get all the answers from it, but to open a dialogue with yourself as to who you are, where you are going, and what your purpose is in life. By seeking out and understanding what you already have, you will make your dreams a reality. It will help you open up the world of possibilities that will inspire you to move beyond making a living to living your life. Will you dare to go beyond your dreams and realize the awesome beauty of what it is to really be you? Will you stand up and take on the grave responsibility for which you were created? When the knock arrives at the door of your heart, will you hear it? It will contain all that you are and all that you can be, waiting for you to dare to go beyond your dreams. Your life is waiting for you to live it.

Together, we will take a journey to define a mission statement for our lives that will help lead, guide, motivate, and inspire us to a commitment level we have never experienced before. Demonstrate to yourself and those around you that you wake each day with the firm decision that your life is driven not by accident, but by purpose and that you look toward tomorrow with positive affirmation, not doubt or apprehension. This is the time to take control of our lives with the necessary commitment and self-control. We must focus on those things that mean the most and that will get us where we want and need to be.

We must look at this impending journey as a brand new vision that will help us break down the negative walls of the past and build walls of positive attitude toward our future. This new vision will break the past chains of limitations, while opening doors of fresh possibilities for tomorrow. This is your firm stance against self-doubt: negative thoughts that try to destroy your hope and dreams. Now is the time to focus on what you want with the positive affirmation that "I Can." Put aside the "How will I?" and hold on to "I know I Can." The realization of your dreams is not as hard as the willingness to define them.

My dad died of prostate cancer on August 24, 1998. His life is captured in his words: "I have lived my life, I have enjoyed my life, I've done in life all that I wanted to do, and now, if I have to die, I am ready." He dared to go beyond his dreams and, in doing so, overcame many obstacles. He made his dreams a reality and left footprints in the sands of time, whereby we know that James Gerald has been here. Will someone be able to say the same about us, or will it be said that we merely lived and died, robbing life of our precious gifts and talents? Let us start now, living our lives with a sense of purpose. Then, when that final day comes, the dash between your date of birth and date of death will signify your life: **You Dared To Go Beyond Your Dreams**.

CHAPTER ONE

IN THE BEGINNING
The Dream

Joseph had a dream... Listen to this dream I had: We were binding sheaves of grain out in the field when suddenly my sheaf rose and stood upright, while your sheaves gathered around mine and bowed down to it . . .
                                                              —Genesis 37:5-7

THE WORLD, OUR country specifically, has been molded and shaped by the actions and lives of those that have gone before us. Those lives have etched their names into history and have left footprints in the sands of time, telling those of us behind them that they have been here. It was their strength and their commitment to achieve their dreams and live out their purpose that have brought us to where we are today and have provided an example for us to follow. It all had to begin with a thought, an idea—the dream. The dreams to be more, to do more and experience more. The dream to live a fulfilled life taking advantage of every opportunity that presented itself. Allow me a few moments to share with you several examples of those that lived their lives making great differences in the way we live our lives today. They came with nothing more than just a dream and a since of purpose. It was their courage, sacrifice and commitment to go beyond just the thoughts of their dreams, which have left behind examples to emulate and have made such great differences in our lives today.

The settling of and building of America began with an idea or if you will a dream—that the citizens of a society could join freely and agree to govern themselves by making laws for the common good. The pilgrims stated:

We whose names are underwritten . . . doe by these presents solemnly and mutually in the presence of God, and one another, covenant and combine ourselves together into a civil body politic.

That was November 11, 1620, after sixty days at sea, the sailing ship Mayflower approached land. On board were 102 passengers. They anchored in what we now know as Provincetown Harbor off of Cape Cod. Although they hadn't reached the mouth of the Hudson River, their original destination, they decided to stay where they were due to rough seas and the fact that they were not in the area for which they had the patent.

Before disembarking, they signed a covenant, the Mayflower Compact, in order to establish a basis for self-government by which all of them were bound. That November day, in a wilderness harbor, the covenant entered into on that ship established the basis for self-government and the rule of law in the new land. It all began with a dream, and an idea that became reality once they dared to put their thoughts into action.

In defense of freedom of the press, Andrew Hamilton once stated, "The loss of liberty to a generous mind is worse than death." Andrew Hamilton was the defense lawyer for John Peter Zenger's who was arrested for seditious libel because he published the *New York Weekly Journal* in 1733, criticizing the policies of the colonial governor. Mr. Zengar was acquitted and his defense by Hamilton was noted as a great victory for freedom of the press. It all began with one person standing up for what he believed in, thereby living out his purpose.

Patrick Henry's speech to the second Virginian Convention went down in history: "I know not what course others may take, but as for me, give me liberty, or give me death." He became a leading patriot in the revolutionary course, which in turn became an advocate of the colonies' rights. Another person, daring to go beyond the status quo to live out his purpose.

Thomas Jefferson's writings of the "Declaration of Independence" helped shape America and make it what it is today:

We hold these truths to be self-evident that all men are created equal, that they are endowed by their Creator with certain unalienable rights, that among these are life, liberty and the pursuit of happiness. . . .

Thomas Jefferson wrote the first draft of the "Declaration of Independence," stating that it was "an appeal to the tribunal of the world." He is a true example of one person making a very big difference and living out his life's purpose.

In 1737, Thomas Paine was born in England to a poor Quaker father and an Anglican mother. He left school at the age of thirteen and immigrated to the colonies in 1774. Paine's famed writings, *Common Sense*, persuaded the public to recognize the need for independence from Britain. He was a testament to his statement: "The harder the conflict, the more glorious the triumph . . ." He sincerely believed that "he whose heart is firm, and whose conscience approves his conduct, will pursue his principles unto death."

In his publication, *Civil Disobedience,* Henry David Thoreau stated: "Under a government which imprisons anyone unjustly, the true place for a just man is also in prison." Thoreau, who refused to pay taxes to a government that permitted slavery and that waged an imperialist war against Mexico, was placed in jail. He wrote his views in the form of a lecture that was published, but did not initially sell. Mohandos K. Gandhi read his writing, was very impressed with Thoreau, and became a lifelong exemplar of civil disobedience and passive resistance to an unjust authority. Gandhi in turn influenced Reverend Dr. Martin Luther King Jr., and Thoreau's ideas found new life as the basic ideology of the American civil rights movement. These are examples of people daring to be themselves and live out their life's purpose for the benefit all.

Sojourner Truth's address to the Ohio Women's Rights Convention is still an inspiration to many today: "And Ain't I a Woman?" She was born into slavery, later released, and was the only black woman in attendance at the 1851 Women's Rights Convention in Akron, Ohio. Many participants objected to her presence, fearing that the feminist cause would get mixed-up with the unpopular abolitionist cause. As she rose to speak, there was a hiss of disapproval, but when she finished, there were roars of applause from the audience. She was yet another person with the commitment and courage to stand up and be heard.

Susan B. Anthony's fight for women's right to vote took America to a new level: "It's we, the people, not we, the white male citizens, nor we, the male citizens, but we, the whole people, who formed this union." Indeed, the rights enjoyed by women today can be attributed to her strength of spirit and character.

Langston Hughes, born in Joplin, Missouri in 1902, was one of the most gifted poets of the Harlem Renaissance. With his writings, "Montage of Dreams Deferred," the African-American activist and gifted writer of black culture inspired others to hold on to their dreams.

The "I Have a Dream" speech, by Reverend Dr. Martin Luther King Jr., became the "American Dream" and the inspiration to make America a place of equality for all. It was a call for America to make good on the "Declaration of Independence." It goes without saying that King helped to ensure the rights of African-Americans and, indeed, society as a whole.

These are but a few of the courageous souls that dared to go beyond their dreams and live out their purposes in life. Because they did, we are much better off as a people and as a nation. The dreams of these individuals have contributed significantly to our current level of equality. They would be proud. Their lives have demonstrated that no matter who we are and where we are in life, we do count—we all are unique, which allows us to contribute something that no one else can provide. We must remember in our hearts that we do matter, and that we can make a difference if only we try.

"Listen to this dream I had." Those six seemingly little words of the young seventeen-year-old Joseph were spoken with excitement and enthusiasm to his family. He dreamt that he would one day become a great leader and that his brothers and even his mother and father would bow to him. Allow me to briefly capture his story and set the stage from which we will proceed.

Joseph, considered a big dreamer by his siblings, was the elder son of Rachel—his father's second wife and first love. His father favored him, which made his ten older brothers jealous, envious, and filled with hatred toward him. Eventually, their anger grew so intense that they plotted to kill their own brother.

One day, while they were working in a faraway land, they saw him approaching from a distance. "Here comes that dreamer. Let's throw him in this pit and see what becomes of his dreams!" They first threw him into the pit without food or water. Then they sold him into slavery for twenty pieces of silver. The brothers took Joseph's coat, daubed it with the blood of a kid goat, and told their father that a wild animal had killed him.

Joseph's captors carried him to Egypt and resold him to Potiphar, a high-ranking captain of the Pharaoh's guard. He became so fond of Joseph that he placed him as head of his household. Some time thereafter, Potiphar's wife accused Joseph of rape because he'd refused to sleep with her. He was thrown into prison where the governor of the prison eventually put him in charge of the other prisoners. While in prison, he met the Pharaoh's chief butler and chief baker, both whom had offended the Pharaoh. Both of them had dreams that they could not understand, so they asked Joseph to interpret their meanings. Joseph honored their request with one of his own. He asked that they keep him in mind once they were free and to tell the Pharaoh that he had hopes for release as well. They agreed and Joseph told them the meaning of their dreams. He told the butler that he would be restored to his office in three days and told the chef that he would be hanged.

The butler, who had promised to tell Pharaoh about Joseph, forgot until two years later—on the day the Pharaoh himself had several disturbing dreams that no one could interpret. The butler then remembered Joseph and told the Pharaoh how Joseph had interpreted his dream of being restored to his position as butler and the chef's dream of being hanged.

The Pharaoh called for Joseph who was able to explain his dreams. The Pharaoh then rewarded Joseph by placing him second in charge of Egypt. The Pharaoh took his signet ring from his finger and put it on Joseph's. He dressed him in robes of fine linens and put a gold chain around his neck. Now second-in-command, Joseph escorted the Pharaoh in his chariot. The daughter of the Egyptian priest was given as his wife.

Famine eventually affected Joseph's father, Jacob, as well as his family and people. Joseph moved his father, family, and people into Egypt.

We can either attribute Joseph's self-assurance to the favorite son status he held with his father or to knowing his purpose in life through the dreams he received from God. Truthfully, Joseph had every right to forsake his dream. He was ridiculed and despised for his dreams, he was betrayed and sold into slavery by his own family, punished for doing the right thing, and went through a long period of imprisonment while those he'd helped to freedom had forgotten him. Despite all this, he knew his purpose and felt self-assurance, molded by his reluctance to let go of his dreams. This understanding allowed him to move beyond the mere thought of his dreams to experience their reality. It allowed him to move beyond the doubt, pain, fears, and sadness in order to achieve his dreams. In the beginning, it all began with a dream.

"Listen to this dream I had." Joseph's words should also be on our lips. Like Joseph, we should also speak them without fear or intimidation. After all, our dreams and purpose in life are at stake. Others will not take us seriously about where we are headed if we ourselves aren't convinced that we know. It is likely that Joseph's brothers became increasingly jealous and envious of him after hearing of his dreams, because he projected confidence about his dreams, his purpose.

It all begins with a thought, an idea, a sense of purpose, and the dream. Not the typical sleep dream, but "The Dream." The dream that answers the age-old questions: Why am I here? What is my purpose in life? The dream that, when achieved, brings you true happiness, joy, and fulfillment. This dream announces to the world that we know who we are, where we came from, and where we are going. The Dream makes us understand exactly how wonderful it is to be us. We are talking about the dream that takes all of our talents, those things we do best, and feeds life's purpose. That dream signifies the real "us" waiting to be released so that we may freely express ourselves. It all starts with The Dream—and it's already there, on the inside, waiting to become reality. I like what Henry David Thoreau said with regards to our dreams— *"If one advances confidently in the direction of His dreams, and endeavors to live the life which he has imagined, he will meet with a success unexpected in common hours."*

The minority persons in this country—and any country, for that matter—are not those that differ in appearance, race, creed, or color; the minority are those that know what they want in life and understand the unique talent they can contribute to this world. Benjamin E. Mays once said:

It must be borne in mind that the tragedy in life doesn't lie in not reaching your goal. The tragedy lies in having no goal to reach. It isn't a calamity to die with dreams unfulfilled, but it is calamity not to dream. It isn't a disaster to be unable to capture your ideal, but it is a disaster to have no ideal to capture. It is not a disgrace not to reach the stars, but it is a disgrace to have no stars to reach. Not failure but low aim is a sin.

His words remind us that it is not so bad to never see your dream to completion; it is only tragic to never have any dreams, hopes, or purpose. The even greater tragedy is having dreams and hopes, but never pressing towards those dreams with the hope of making them a reality.

Just as we work to make a living, we must work even harder to have a life. We spend so much time worrying about making a living that soon we realize we have no life. We are alive, but not living; we wake to go to work and come home, eat, watch television, and maybe talk to friends. We hurry off to bed to get up in the morning and return to work to pay the bills. Then we come home and repeat the cycle. Somewhere and somehow, we decided that making a living came before having a life. We have, in a sense, sold our dreams, our lives, in order to make a living. Until we decide we won't sell our souls by just earning a living and choose to pursue a life instead, we can never truly achieve the kind of

success that gives life meaning and purpose. In other words, a successful life is not determined by how we make a living, but in how we live.
Making a daily living can consume us so completely that we lose focus
of who we are and what we really want to do with our lives. Our dreams
become secondary and we become uncomfortable with who we are and
where we are in life's journey. It is because of this discomfort that many
of us have felt in our hearts, there *is* more to life than what we experience each day. Your dreams hold the key to the "more" in life; they hold
the key to a successful and fulfilling life.

Look around you. All that you see began in someone's mind.
Someone had to step beyond the initial thought to make all that you
see around you reality. Take a drive around your neighborhood and
you will soon realize the dreams made real by ordinary people just like
you and I. You may see Wal-Mart, the dream of Mr. Sam Walton who
opened the first of a chain of Ben Franklin five-and-dime franchises in
Arkansas, and in 1962, his first Wal-Mart discount store. In 1991 Wal-
Mart became the nation's largest retailer, with 1,700 stores; he was
reported by Forbes to be the richest man in the country. Then there's
Marriott Hotels, Mr. John Marriott's dream. Mr. Marriott's first Hot
Shoppe in Washington, D.C. quickly grew into a chain of family-style
drive-ins. Marriott Corporation became a major U.S. hospitality company after diversifying into airline catering and motels. There's the
Renaissance Hotels and TGI Friday's restaurants by Mr. Carlson.
There's also The Microsoft Corporation, which changed the way we do
business. This was the dream of Mr. Bill Gates. This Skinny, shy and
awkward, teenaged Bill Gates seemed an unlikely successor to his over-
achieving parents. His father, powerfully built and 6'6" tall, was a
prominent Seattle attorney, and his gregarious mother served on char-
itable boards and ran the United Way. While he showed enormous talent for math and logic, young Bill, a middle child, was no one's idea
of a natural leader, let alone a future billionaire who would reinvent
American business. Then there's Mr. Dell, the dreamer behind the
Dell computer. At age eight, Dell sent away for equivalency testing to
earn his high school diploma. In 1984, nineteen-year-old University of
Texas freshman Michael Dell had a simple idea. Why not sell custom-
made computers directly to customers? At the time, computer manufacturers sold their machines wholesale to retailers, who marked up
the price for consumers. Instead, Dell assembled computers from

cheap surplus parts, then created souped-up machines to the specifications of his customers. By the time he started college, his parents were beginning to worry about his grades, so he promised he would quit his computer venture and devote himself to the books if his business didn't perform well. But by the end of the year, the company was making $50,000-$80,000 a month. Dell incorporated his business and dropped out of college. Fifteen years later, the simple idea is still working. Dell's still doing essentially the same thing—supplying made-to-order computers directly to customers—but on a scale that now brings in $18 billion a year with 25,000 employees. Dell's breathtaking success made him, at age twenty-seven, the youngest CEO of a Fortune 500 company in history, and *Fortune* magazine named his company one of the most-admired firms in America, following G.E., Coca-Cola, and Microsoft. The list goes on and on. What do all these individuals have in common? They are all individuals, just like us, but they dared to make their dreams reality. They took the first steps and moved their dreams from perception into action.

It is far easier to live our lives through the fulfilled dreams and achievements of others rather than living our own dreams. We can spend the whole day seeing, touching, and feeling the dreams of others made real, but when will someone see our dreams as reality? In Romans 12:6-8, the Bible says:

"We have different gifts, according to the grace given us. If a man's gift is prophesying, let him use it in proportion to his faith; if it is serving, let him serve; if it is teaching, let him teach; if it is encouraging, let him encourage, if it is contributing to the needs of others, let him give generously; if it is leadership, let him govern diligently; if it is showing mercy, let him do it cheerfully.

These gifts are truly the foundation of our dreams and these dreams are our purpose for living. We exist so that we can contribute to our world, to use our gifts to help others, and to use that unique gift to live a fulfilled life. In other words, our special gifts and unique talents are the answers to what our life's true purpose may be. The lack of purpose produces emptiness, goals without fulfillment, and achievements without joy.

I must reiterate that the Scripture from Romans reminds us that God did not give everybody everything, but he did give everybody something. That something is the reason you were born and is your purpose in life. If you understand that very important truth, you have achieved the beginning, or have taken the first step, of going beyond your dream. Some of us were given the ability to love, some to speak, some to listen, some to preach and some to teach, some to sing and some to dance, some to destroy and some to build up, some to practice and some to play. Regardless of your gift, it is all yours. It is the expression of that something that separates us. It separates the professional from the amateur, the great from the small, the gifted from the not so gifted, the happy from the sad.

It is that special something, that gift, that moves Michael Jordan to great heights and Anita Baker to wonderful notes. It writes the words of Maya Angelo and speaks the words of John F. Kennedy. It inspires the pen of Langston Hughes and gives courage to the passion inside Dr. Martin Luther King. That gift marched with Colin Powell and it created America through its people. These people love what they do (or did), not because of monetary gifts, but because it is their expression of the gift given to them by the Creator. They have decided to take on not just a career, but their purpose in life. Instead of just advancing in a dead-end job, they blossomed in the gifts that were freely bestowed on them. They dared to go beyond their dreams to live out their purpose in life.

I am not saying that our jobs are not important. They are necessary for paying the bills, but it is our gifts and talents that should help us decide where we belong in life, what our purpose is in life, and how we should make a living. The career we choose should be based on the purpose we have for our lives rather than the amount of money we can make. Unlike a job, a career based on purpose is what you want to do, like to do, love doing, and are excited about doing. It should be in alignment with who you are, rather than you aligning yourself with what you do. If we can achieve this, we will then be able to greet our mornings with a sense of purpose rather than the despair of repetitiveness.

When we put a career ahead of our passion, we begin to chase, instead of purpose, the tangible things in life such as fame, money, and wealth. We all know that money cannot buy happiness. Many supposedly successful people express an uncomfortable feeling of emptiness and try to fill it with material goods. We cannot rely on objects to make ourselves happy. Only we can do that. The drive born out of purpose will be much greater than the drive birthed from money, power, and social status. Once you choose a career or way of life that correlates with your talents and gifts, you will notice not only the professional awards, but also the personal awards of achievement and fulfillment. I, too, would like to be rich and successful, but I ultimately prefer a sense of purpose to monetary wealth.

Without our dream, however, we can never truly know success or understand our purpose. It must first begin with The Dream. If we have already achieved our dreams or are progressing toward making them a reality, we can be labeled as successful in the truest sense of the word. Essentially, we can measure success by determining whether we are doing what we feel we are meant to do, achieving our own personal goals in life, and making our dream a reality. Again, success cannot be measured in monetary value and the amount of our worldly possessions, only in how we feel about our achievements and ourselves at the end of the day. If we can get up each day, do what we do, and be happy with our lives, then we have achieved a certain level of success. When we see ourselves fulfilling our purpose and contributing to this world, then we will know that we have reached a certain degree of success.

That success is created by intangible things. That success is evident in the top executives who are the best at what they do and know that that is their purpose. It's just as apparent in the janitor who is happy with his work and does it well. Without this measure of success, we will settle for just another position, job, or paycheck rather than living out our true purpose. We'll only be "making a living."

It all begins with The Dream and knowing that there is more to life than who and what we have become. It begins with the dream that pervades all our thoughts, the drive that takes over our feelings and emotions, and makes us who we really are.

Just as Joseph had a dream, I believe that we all have dreams about what we most want to do in life. With those dreams comes great determination as well as a deep, yearning desire, which, if left unacknowledged, will make us feel that something is missing from our lives. We'll feel empty, that there should be much more to our lives than what we are doing. It is important to note that Joseph could never have achieved his dreams unless he actually believed that he could. He had to hold his dreams in his mind and heart instead of dismissing them as ridiculous or impossible. It is too easy to dismiss our dreams because of what others might say, what we have or the lack thereof, the fear of failure, or how impossible it may seem to achieve such a dream.

Look at Joseph, just a farm boy with twelve brothers. He did not appear to be anyone special; nothing about him was noteworthy. However, he had a dream that he would one day be a ruler, the president if you will. He did not have a substantial education, he was not from a royal family, and he was not wealthy. Furthermore, everyone he shared his dreams with dismissed him as being ridiculous. Everything about him said that his dreams were out of his reach. Still, he believed in himself and his dreams; with the higher power working within him, his odds were later turned around. We find out later in this story that Joseph will continue to move closer to his dream and will no longer be a farm boy, but the ruler of Egypt. Joseph had more than just a dream. He had the courage to go after that dream and become a great leader.

In Chapter 25 of Matthew, Jesus tells a parable of a man going on a journey. He left his property in the care of his servants, giving three of them a certain amount of money. The servant with the most money put it to work and doubled what he had. The servant that received the second most money did the same thing and doubled what he had. The servant with the least amount of money did the least with what he had. Instead of using what he had to gain more, he hid it in the ground.

After the man returned home from his long journey, he asked the servants to explain what they had done with what he had given them. The two servants who received the most told him that they put the money to work and it doubled. The man told the servants that they had done good and been faithful with what they had; therefore, they would be in charge of even more money in the future. The third servant told the man that he'd hid his money because he was afraid of losing the little he had. He returned to the master exactly what he had received. The master became upset and told him that rather than hiding it, he should have used what he had so that it could grow. The man then ordered that the servant be taken away from him.

This parable directly correlates to our lives—we have all received something from God. Like the first two men, we should spend our time using what we have received in order to find our purpose and live a fulfilled life. If, instead, we choose not to use that special gift, then it will be lost. What a travesty to go through life afraid to use the instruments of our life's purpose.

It is relatively easy to come up with a dream and to conceive the amount of work necessary to make it a reality. The next step is not so easy. It requires confidence, commitment, and a sense of focus. We will have to labor and toil with much sweat to make that dream a reality, but our reward will be the sense of purpose and control we have over our lives. We will have to use what we have internally to overcome the many valleys and obstacles ahead, but eventually we can soar with our wings, looking down over the valley of obstacles, past our mistakes, and alleviate our fears.

Some look back at yesterday and regret what could have been. Some look at tomorrow with fear of making changes or sacrificing for what they really want. Too many move through their days without vision for tomorrow.

Think about what you want to get out of life. Think about your dream. Is the thought of achieving this dream so strong that you, like Joseph, are willing to declare first to yourself and then through your actions that you will achieve that dream? Is the purpose of your dream important enough that you are willing to, with confidence, sacrifice common opinion and possible comfort to stand up for what you believe and want?

We hold these truths to be self evident, that all men are created equal and endowed, by their Creator, with certain inalienable rights. Those rights are life, liberty and the pursuit of happiness.

Even in the beginning of this great nation, those that coined the "Declaration of Independence" recognized that we all have a great desire to freely express our dreams. They supported our right to do whatever we want with our lives as long as it does not infringe upon others' pursuit of happiness. They also recognized that, courtesy of our Creator, we all have what it takes to make our dreams a reality and live out our purpose. That declaration affords all of us the freedom to use our unique talents to achieve our dreams and live out a life full of purpose. In recognition of this truth, many people throughout our history have used the words of the Declaration of Independence to inspire, motivate, teach, and to urge others to remember the basic liberties we all have. We must, however, have the confidence to go after our purpose instead of a promotion, life instead of just a living. We must live our lives according to our talents and not our careers. The Declaration of Independence empowers through the law, God empowers us through the actual dream, but we must empower ourselves with awareness and self-belief.

The beginning must start with us, what we want in life, what we believe, and the way we think about life's issues. What will be our crowning achievement? What will make us a success, not by the world's standards, but by how we define success? How far are we willing to go to achieve it? Only those of us that step from the boardwalk of complacency onto the sands of possibility can leave behind footprints to show that we have been here and for others to follow.

Our goals should be those things that we know will result not just in happiness, but an added sense of achievement and purpose in our lives. Happiness comes and goes with each step we decide to take, but when we define success and accomplishment and actually live it, we have given ourselves a sense of purpose and fulfillment.

Our dreams, our purpose in life may not be one that will put us in history books, on television, or in the newspapers, but more important than fame and fortune is the reward that it brings us and the joy it gives others. We are at our peak when we contribute our talents to something that we believe in. When we isolate our unique talents, we identify those things that come easily to us and that we enjoy doing. Before we go on, we must be clear about what is important to us, what we want to achieve in life, and what we want said about us after we are long gone.

It all starts with a dream, and if we can dream it, we have what it takes to achieve it. Once we start acting on that dream, that something we were given, we will see that all of our life experiences will assist us in reaching for that dream. Furthermore, we can go beyond that dream to living out our purpose in life, today. John Dryden says it like this;

> *Happy the man, and happy he alone,*
> *He who can call today his own;*
> *He who, secure within, can say,*
> *Tomorrow, do they worst, for I have lived today.*

Once we dare to dream, it should be apparent that there is no better time than today to start becoming all that we can and should be.

CHAPTER TWO

TODAY

No Better Time

CONFIDENCE

Then he had another dream, and he told it to his brothers. "Listen," he said, "I had another dream, and this time the sun and the moon and eleven stars were bowing down to me."

—Genesis 37:9

THE CALL CAME while I was in my office Friday afternoon. It was my sister on the other end of the phone. "Dennis," she said, "I believe you need to come now. Daddy is back in the hospital and this time it does not look good for him." I heard the agony, pain, and sense of urgency in her voice. My father had been suffering from prostate cancer and he seemed, at one point, to be getting better. My father: a good husband and great businessman. He was loved by many, and now he was ill and preparing to cross over from life to death. This reality came hard to many of us. Just months earlier, he had danced with my new bride at our Virginia wedding, and we had celebrated his birthday only two months earlier. Today it became undeniably real. We were losing him.

Saturday August 22, 1998, after a five-hour drive from our home in Virginia, my wife, children, and I arrived in Queens, New York around 5:00 p.m. We stopped by my parents' home to find no one there. We went around the corner to my aunt's house to get information about my father's condition and directions to the hospital. We called the hospital and learned that visiting hours would end in approximately two hours. My first thought was that I had every reason to wait until first thing in the morning to go to the hospital. We had just driven over five hours; we were tired and hungry. Nevertheless, the decision was made to go right away and see how he was doing.

We arrived to find my mother and three sisters with him. Things appeared to be just fine. My sisters were joking and my father was calling them clowns and my mother seemed to be taking things in her usual calm fashion. My dad asked my sisters and me to pray with him.

Dear Father,
Here we are now, with our heads bowed down and our hearts reaching toward Heaven to the only name we know, our Father. We want to take time now to thank you for all that you have done for us and through us. Thank you for our eyes that were able to see the sun one more day. Dear Father, as we are now joined this day, hand and hand, heart and heart, agreeing one with another, we ask that you look down on us and take out all that is displeasing in your

sight. Come down now Father and touch our father and husband who lay here on his bed of affliction. Send your angels to be his pillow of peace and your Holy Spirit to comfort him in the midst of his pain. Have favor on him, dear Lord. We know that you are able to heal him at any moment and ask that your divine will now take over. We love you, and we commend this one James Gerald in your hands that you may carry out your will. In the name of Jesus we pray.

Amen.

After prayer, he said, "You just do not know how good it is to you all." He had not slept for some time now and his pain was increasing in intensity. We asked the nurse for his pain medication so that he could get some rest.

My youngest sister would be staying the night with him, so I bid him good night when visiting hours ended. I leaned over, kissed him, and said, "I love you and will see you tomorrow morning." However, when the next morning—Sunday—arrived, he had already slipped into a deep sleep. He never woke up. At about 8:00 p.m. on Monday evening, he stopped breathing and crossed over from us in the physical life to God in the eternal life.

This man I called my father, this one that only five months earlier danced at my wedding, was now gone. I can't help but think that if I had waited until the next day to visit, I would not have had the opportunity to see him, talk with him, pray with him, and tell him that I loved him. That day was the day. I could not imagine my self-inflicted guilt if I had not gone to the hospital when I did, if I had given into the procrastination of waiting until tomorrow instead of doing it today. I would not trade those last moments spent with him for anything, yet those moments would have been lost if I had put off going to the hospital. It was more apparent to me than ever that tomorrow holds no guarantees, and that we should not put off till tomorrow what we can and should do today.

We're all guilty, as are those around us, of saying, "I'll do it tomorrow. I will take care of it tomorrow. I will write that book tomorrow. I will do better tomorrow. I will put together that business plan tomorrow. I will make time for that tomorrow." Tomorrow is so easy to say when we are faced with what needs to be done today. Tomorrow comes and still we have not committed ourselves to do what we said we would do. We soon realize that what we wanted to do—and know we should have done—

slips away, because too many tomorrows have passed. Consequently, we have turned our tomorrows into our yesterdays; the great things we wanted to do have become distant memories or fading dreams.

We sometimes use tomorrow to define our happiness. In other words, we believe that when tomorrow comes, we will be much happier and better off: When I get the bills paid off, I will start this business; once I graduate from school, I will do this; when I get married, I'll do that; when I get divorced, I will have more time to do whatever. When those things happen, we find something else to help us postpone happiness and success. We get out of school, but we don't have any money, because we paid all our bills and we got married, so now we have to wait to get a better job, and when we get a better job, we have more bills. Get the picture? There is no better time than right now to start living your life, because there will always be some obstacle in front you. Life is an obstacle. If we wait until tomorrow, when there are no more obstacles, to live full lives, we just may find out, that our time runs out long before the obstacles will.

Another day passes. We find ourselves putting off things that we could have taken care of today, leaving more room tomorrow for other things. We're likely to find ourselves in this situation because we are overwhelmed by all that we have to accomplish in twenty-four hours. Therefore, we procrastinate. Edward Young says that— *"Procrastination is the thief of time."* We can also become so overwhelmed with the actual thought of what needs to be done to obtain our dreams that we continue to put them off. Again, we procrastinate. Procrastination has become a slayer of dreams for many, because we use it as a crutch not to do or pursue challenging things—things that are important to us and vital for our happiness and fulfillment.

Listen to this dream I have: "I will become CEO/President of our company and everyone will work for me." Once I had this dream, I decided that now was the time to hold on to it and not let go. I decided that today I would tell someone about who I am and who I am to become. I will begin to live, walk, and talk as though I am CEO/President. I am more than what you see before you. I will take the necessary steps to guide me from thought to reality, from perception to purpose. I have decided that today is the day. This is what Joseph said when he received and accepted his dream and embraced what he would become in life.

Joseph gives his brothers three reasons to dislike him. First, he tattles on them. Second, their father openly loves Joseph more than them. Third, Joseph has two dreams, which his brothers interpret as arrogant and egotistical—the younger brother will have authority over his older brothers. Even his father is taken aback by Joseph's second dream—that he and his wife will also bow down to Joseph one day. Could Joseph not anticipate that sharing his dreams would inevitably produce antagonism? It's likely that Joseph, at the young age of seventeen, did not think it through that far. He was simply sharing the sense of destiny that God is opening up before him with anybody who will listen. He is, in a sense, announcing to himself and the world what he is to become.

Joseph took no time waiting to tell people about the dreams he had. There was no tomorrow for Joseph; he was excited and wanted others to know it today. He wasn't boastful, only excited about his dreams. The power of purpose will have that effect on us. Once we have found that thing in life that we should be doing to realize our full potential and purpose, not only will we be eager to start working toward our goals, we will also want to tell the world. Mary Wollstonecraft Shelley says this, with regard to purpose— *"Nothing contributes so much to tranquilize the mind as a steady purpose—a point on which the soul may fix its intellectual eye."*

Nevertheless, it is difficult to tell others about your dreams or your purpose in life if you are not confident in yourself. You must believe that you can achieve those dreams and that your purpose is valid. Joseph was confident and assured that his dreams were his purpose in life because God gave them to him. Again, he had every reason to dismiss his dreams because of the circumstances of his present life, but something inside him must have confirmed that he needed to become more than he already was. This gave him the courage to boldly tell others that he would one day become a great ruler, although he was just a young farm boy. When he decided to share his dreams with others, he stood boldly behind his purpose and knew that that day was the day to start making his dreams a reality. Believe in yourself and then stand with firm determination, knowing that your self-confidence will help you begin living out your purpose today.

I, too, have had self-doubts about why I should not pursue my dream of writing this book. I could easily have listed a myriad of excuses: It will fail, it will be too hard to write, and it will be impossible to get it published. I could also decide that because I am not where I want to be in life, I should ignore my dream of publishing a book until I am in better position. While writing this book, I have come through an extremely difficult time. I have fought a long and hard custody battle, I lost my dad, and I have been diagnosed with Graves' disease. I am working out of financial ruin: I lost a job, had no money in the bank, and was concerned where our next meal would come from and where we would live without income. I had every reason to say that this is not a good time to start working on my dream. However, I understand that my dream is my purpose in life and although today may not be the best time to start, perhaps tomorrow will hold even tougher challenges and the cycle would continue; I would be deferring my dream until my circumstances improved, just to realize that those circumstances are replaced by new ones.

Without commitment to our purpose in life, we will just drift through life, accepting everything that happens and settling for anything as long as it pays the bills and we are getting by. If we accept that, we will lose the ability to dream and the courage to achieve our dreams. Our dreams will become only a memory and a passing thought while our purpose will conform to what we do, instead of what we do being shaped by our purpose.

Joseph wasn't the only one who could have made excuses for giving up on his dreams. All of those mentioned earlier, Thomas Jefferson, Susan B. Anthony, Sojourner Truth, Patrick Henry, John F. Kennedy, Dr. Martin Luther King Jr., Langston Hughes, Michael Jordan, Sam Walton, Bill Gates, and Jesus Christ, could have denied their purposes in life by creating excuses. One or the other could have said that the country is not ready to hear about women voters or equal rights for all people; that the "Declaration of Independence" would not be accepted because of the disbelief that all people are created equal; that they would be persecuted or even killed trying to bring about change in their country. I, personally, have been told that I do not have what it takes to be great and that my writings will never be accepted. But if I accepted that to be the final answer to my life, then they would have been right. However, I have the last word and it is up to me to determine how high I will go and how far I will travel to reach my goals.

There are many reasons the above people have for why they *should not,* but so many more for why they *should.* Just one reason why they should follow their dreams drove them all to make tremendous sacrifices, some even to the point of physical harm. That one reason gave them confidence in their beliefs and commitment to their cause. That one reason was purpose. Everything in them drove them to live out their purpose no matter what the cost, and the cost was very great for the majority of them.

The same applies to all of us: Our purpose moves us to confidence and that in turn must drive us to commitment. Without that purpose, there can be no confidence in where we are going and no commitment to why we are here. We must be driven by our sense of purpose. Once we have that sense of purpose, tomorrow will be too late and today will be just right for doing what we should be doing. We must ask ourselves, "If not today, then when?""If not us, then who?" We as people, and as a country, would not have come nearly so far if those that came before us had made excuses for not doing what they felt they should do.

Many of us find ourselves saying "tomorrow," because the task at hand seems larger than the time we have today or our circumstances are not what we want them to be. However, if we take that task and break it down, we can start achieving today. We may not get it all done today, but when tomorrow comes, we are closer to it than yesterday. I say again, in order to obtain our dreams, we must decide that today we will start living our lives instead of just making a living: "Today is the day that I will start living my dream instead of just thinking about it. Today is the day that I will start pressing toward the reality, rather than dwelling on the impossibility, of my dreams. Today is the day that I will decide to be the very best that I can be by daring to go beyond my dreams and start living out my purpose."

Today, somewhere in the world, people will succeed and people will fail; people will live and people will die; people will build and people will break down. Today, we have chosen to take the first of many steps toward our dreams. Take time now, to affirm what you can and will do today. Today, we will affirm our dedication to living out our life's purpose. Today, I will take advantage of another day to leave my footprints in the sands of time. Today is the day that I move closer to realizing through my dreams how wonderful it is to be me. Today, there is no better time to blossom right where I am. Today, I will live the life that I know I should. Today.

The dream is extremely powerful; the thoughts of our dreams can excite us while the achievements of our dreams can challenge us. If we do not commit to them, the dreams will remain only thoughts in our heads, and the "could be," "can be," and "should be" statements will be the marquees of our lives.

The fear of failing or taking a chance is likely the number one reason so many of us defer our dreams and put off achieving our goals. We will sometimes defer our dreams because of that fear, and we will trade them in for what we think is security, but is nothing more than complacency. Those with vision and purpose will dare to take the risks necessary to achieve and go beyond their dreams. They will take on the obstacles of today and the unknowns of tomorrow. Unless we have the confidence to take on the challenges of achieving our dreams and our purpose, the answers to why we are here will be hidden. We must view our dreams with the assurance that we have what it takes on the inside to live out our purpose and make those dreams reality. With this confidence, we can come face to face with those age-old questions: What is my purpose? Why am I here?

Once you have that confidence, you are then willing to dare to be who you are, accept responsibility for where you are, endure during the rough times, remain persistent in the midst of the negative times, break down walls of self-doubt, and build the walls of positive thinking. It is confidence that will help you unveil and take advantage of the possibilities, but not dwell on the impossibilities. Confidence will help you see what you can do with what you have rather than what you cannot do with what you do not have.

If we look around, we can easily see that confidence is the key ingredient missing from those that do not achieve or reach their full potential; when it is present, we will find people daring to live out their purpose. Lack of confidence is evident in the words of those who give reasons for not even trying to go for their dreams. You will hear them say:

"I just want to get my pension."

"Starting a business requires a whole lot of time and money that I don't have."

"Over half of start-up businesses fail within the first two to three years."

"I'm not smart enough."

"My vote is only one vote and does not matter."

"They will never listen to me anyway."

"Someone else is probably already doing that."

"If it's such a good idea, why hasn't someone else thought of it?"

Dr. Martin Luther King Jr. once said, *"If a man hasn't discovered something that he will die for, he isn't fit to live."* That confidence is the key to making your life worth something by standing up for what you believe in.

I believe that, even if people are stripped of everything, they can still have a positive attitude and believe in themselves if their confidence, that confidence which is born out of belief in purpose and faith in God, remains intact. They can hold on to their identities, endure, and remain persistent. Once a person's confidence is broken, the spirit is broken. Naturally, the person is as well.

Today, the first day of 2000, I looked at television and realized that so much time has slipped by. It seemed as if the music and movies I use to enjoy were from just last year; in reality, they were from fifteen years ago. My memories of yesterday were not from yesterday, but several years ago. What have I to show for all of these years I have lived? I must decide here and now, today is the day. There is no better time for me to start living my life and stop allowing life to pass me by or to just happen. Today, I will be courageous and take advantage of each day that life gives me. Today, I will set goals and establish plans to achieve them. Today, I will step out of procrastination, out of "It's your fault I am where I am," the self-pity mentality, and into the "I will," and "I can" mentality. I want to look back on this year with a sense of accomplishment and fulfillment. I will take on the courage today and decide to make the most of each day while I Dare to Go Beyond My Dreams. I have decided to get to know me and to be who I am, right where I am. Today, I have decided to move beyond the past, to live for today so that I will be closer to my goals tomorrow. Listen to what Robert Jones Burdette said about living life for today; *"There are two days in the week about which and upon which I never worry. Two carefree days, kept sacredly free from fear and apprehension. One of those days is yesterday... And the other day I do not worry about is tomorrow."*

This poem from an unknown author says it all and concludes this chapter:

I may never see tomorrow; there's no written guarantee,
And things that happened yesterday belong to history.
I cannot predict the future, I cannot change the past,
I have just the present moment, I must treat it as my last.

I must use this moment wisely for it soon will pass away,
And be lost to me forever as part of yesterday.
I must exercise compassion, help the fallen to their feet,
Be a friend unto the friendless, make an empty life complete.

The unkind things I do today may never be undone,
And friendships that I fail to win may nevermore be won.
I may not have another chance on bended knee to pray,
And thank God with humble heart for giving me this day.

—Author Unknown

Today, I will dare to go beyond the thoughts of my dreams to realizing exactly how wonderful it is, to be me.

[CHAPTER THREE]

BE WHO YOU IS, NOT WHO YOU AIN'T

Identity

"ALWAYS BE TRUE TO YOURSELF"

Joseph had a dream, and when he told it to his brothers, they hated him all the more. Then he had another dream. . . . When he told his father as well as his brothers . . . His brothers were jealous of him. . . .
—Genesis 37:5,9,10

GROWING UP IN the South, there was an old saying I used to hear. I believe it originated from a song, then became a sort of rhyme: "Be who you is and not who you ain't, for when you is what you ain't, you ain't what you is." In other words, when we try to be something that we are not, we become something that we really are not. We must come to understand how wonderful it is to be who we are. That is to say, until we discover our wings, we have no real purpose in life. Until we learn how to soar above our fears and doubts and pursue our dreams, we will fail to understand the great privilege it is to be us and will never know who we really are. "Be who you is and not who you ain't, for when you is what you ain't, you ain't what you is."

I can identify with what Joseph went through with his brothers and, at the same time, what his brothers felt. They were jealous of him and had been from the beginning, when they learned of Joseph's favorite-son status with their father. To intensify their jealousy, he then had a dream that he would one day be a great ruler. Their jealousy grew to hatred and they decided to get rid of him. In the beginning, his brothers started out only wanting what Joseph had. After Joseph shared his dreams, they decided that Joseph shouldn't have anything. When we look at what others have, we can lose track of what we have and lose ourselves in someone else's life. This is what happened to Joseph's brothers; in trying to live Joseph's life, they forgot who they were. They may not have had the favorite-son status, but each one of them had his special place. It is dangerous to get wrapped up in what others have, because, like Joseph's brothers, you start looking at what you do not have and begin to think yourself less than others. This kind of thinking alters the way we act and react in life.

It is amazing the lengths we will go to to be like someone else or to hide what we are in order to be something that we are not. We will overextend ourselves to drive a car like someone else's. We will do whatever it takes to live in the largest house and dress in clothes that we cannot afford, or may not even like, just to impress others. We will go through life trying to keep up with everyone else or trying to impress people we don't like or really know. Too many of us spend our lives imitating others—or being something other than ourselves—because of jealousy or the fear that others won't like us for ourselves. It is unfortunate that some choose to identify others' status and fine possessions with success, thereby measuring their own worth in comparison.

It has taken me a long time to really know myself and who I am: my likes and dislikes, what I stand for, and most importantly, what I want and where I am going in life. At one time, I adopted the identity of those I either wanted to be or those that I was envious of. I took on an identity that I thought others wanted to see so they could look up to me. I achieved this by talking like others; acting or saying what others would say; and even lying about who I was, my achievements, and where I came from. I did not see any wrong in this. People do it all the time. I was subtle and no one was any the wiser. I lived these lies for some time; when the present lie ran out, I quickly adapted to my surroundings once again, trying to be what I thought others wanted me to be or what I thought would gain praise from others. This went on for so long that I never really knew who I was. What was my outlook on life? How did I feel about certain issues? What were my true dreams?

My lies may have impressed others, but I only felt confusion and self-doubt in my life, true abilities, and purpose. How could I not? Trying to be like others and keeping the lies straight expends valuable energy. Furthermore, one great lie after another left me beginning to believe the lies myself. I was depriving others and myself of knowing the real me—good, bad, or indifferent. I became so wrapped up in impressing and not disappointing others that I became a big disappointment to myself—I realized I did not know who I was. Eventually, the ones I tried most to impress or not disappoint were the ones that were most disappointed and hurt. I would have gained the very thing I sought most by just being myself. It was the real me that people grew to know and love.

One of the people I most looked up to and admired was the Reverend Dr. Martin Luther King Jr. I was so moved by this great man: the way he was able to command attention with his words, the masterful way in which he wrote, and his ability to move people to action. I knew that I wanted what he had, and I was going to try and capture that in myself. I wanted to be just like Dr. King. I began to read his autobiographies and study and memorize his speeches and sermons. I began to practice his speeches; because I have a very deep voice, I already sounded a little like him. I took advantage of every occasion to use my newfound talents. I would lead black history programs and Dr. King observance programs, fine tuning myself into this role. People would comment on how wonderful I was and how much I reminded them of Dr. King. They were actually complimenting Dr. King, not me. I did not see that initially. It had not yet occurred to me that I really did not want to be Dr. King; I just wanted the courage to use my talents like he did and to live out my purpose in life. As I learned later, I wanted to be recognized for who I was and for my own accomplishments. No matter how much I tried be like him, the only thing that will matter at the end of the day is what I have achieved in my own right. I did not want to be known for being a great imitator of Dr. King. Do not get me wrong; I do believe his principles in life are worth emulating, but we must each use our own gifts to make a difference as he did. That does not mean imitating his actions, but following his example. He should be regarded as a mentor—someone to motivate and inspire you to be the best that you can be.

My wake-up call came once I accepted my calling into the ministry. It was time for me to step up and take on the leadership role as pastor of my first church. A young lady in the congregation made a remark to the outgoing pastor that Reverend Drake was a wonderful man who gives very good sermons, but she wasn't sure he was "real" when speaking. You see, this young lady was not bringing into question my speaking ability or my teachings, but she was questioning my sincerity. What a wake-up call! At first, I was angry and defensive: What right does she have to question my sincerity? Then I was humbled and a little embarrassed. She had every right to demand to know me and not know who I tried to be. People can often tell, if they look closely enough, whether you are genuine or pretending to be someone else. I was trying so hard to be someone else that even I did not recognize the real me.

Once I took on the challenge of being me, I realized that God had gifted me with a powerful voice that can command attention as well as a loving heart and great determination and true sincerity to make a difference in the world around me. People appreciated me for me. It also turns out that Dr. King and I do have a very similar preaching style, so I am told.

What a wonderful discovery at that time in my life. It helped me to see who I really am and to know that I can be myself without fear of what others might think. It gave me the confidence to stand on my own merits and special gifts. It gave me the opportunity to accept myself for who I am and not measure myself against what others have or the status of others. It also taught me that I do not have to be envious of what others have or where they are in their lives, because although God may not have given us everything that others have, he gave us something unique. We must take hold of that something in order to reveal our true identity.

I cannot be the man that Dr. King was nor can I do what he did just as Dr. King could not be the man that I am or accomplish my purpose in life. I may be able talk like him, act like him, and perhaps even look like him, but I can never be him. The awesome truth of the matter is that there is more to him, and all of us, than what people see on the outside: the way we talk, the way we walk, and the way we look and act.

We are products of our past and present environment, experiences, our relationships, and all the things we had to live through. Our experiences in life provide the unique qualities that make us who we are and equip us for what we need in order to go beyond our dreams. It is our experiences in life, good or bad, our childhood follies, our work experiences, our relationships, and our personal history that come together to make us the unique individuals that we are. These experiences that have molded our qualities are the ones that we must come face to face with, because they are the reasons we do the things we do. We must identify our qualities and work on strengthening them.

When we try to be someone else, it is very difficult to see what we need to do within ourselves to reach and go beyond our dreams. When we try to be something that we are not or become jealous of others, we are, in a sense, voiding all that we have gone through in our lives, thus erasing our history—the very thing that shapes and molds our future. Most importantly, we are doing a disservice to God and ourselves by not using our inherent abilities to their capacity.

Jesus said in Matthew 23 that there are those that work hard to make themselves look good on the outside, but the inside is a mess. He says that we should work on ourselves from the inside and that the outside will then be in order. Once we have looked at ourselves from within and understand who we are and where we are gong, the outside will show that same confidence that comes from knowing that our life has a purpose. We cannot work on ourselves from the inside if we are trying hard to disguise our outside or mold ourselves after others or something that we are not.

Permit me to clarify this a bit. The things I have experienced in my life have made who I am. The friends I have made, the household in which I was raised, my interaction with my siblings, places I've been, and the people I've met have impacted me in one way or another. Because these things have contributed to making me who I am today, they are factors in the decisions I make and my reactions to situations. Knowing that, it stands to reason that I am unique, and the way I act or react will never be identical to anyone else. The manner in which I preach and the philosophy I have on life will be molded out of my very own experiences. When I tried to become someone else, I was in turn suppressing my experiences and trying to take on the character of that person. It is extremely difficult to work on yourself when you are trying to be someone else. It is hard to focus on your own beliefs and philosophy when you are trying to live someone else's life. No matter how well I did, I could never truly be like that person, because I could never walk in his shoes or experience life the way he did. When Dr. Martin Luther King Jr. delivered the "I Have a Dream" speech, it could never be repeated as he said it; the eloquence and strength of its delivery was based on his life and experiences. I wanted to emulate him, but I could not become him.

God has taken the time to plant each of us where we are. It is up to us to grow, where God has planted us, into what God has provided and to be the very best we can be. We have what it takes on the inside to achieve whatever our minds perceive. I heard it once said, with minor alterations from me:

If you can't be a pine on top of the hill, then be a shrub in the valley. If you can't be a moon, then be the star, but be the best that you are. If you can't be a highway, then be a trail. It is not by size that you win or fail, not by gender male or female, but by what is inside of you.

In other words, we must use what we have and where we are in life, dedicating ourselves to being the very best that we are.

Try not to limit your accomplishments to what others have done, because it will detract you from focusing on yourself and will lead to discouragement. We cannot measure our successes according to the standards of others. When we start looking at what we have, chances are we'll find the formula for success already planted inside of us. Let's take time to set the standards for our own lives and not worry about how we measure up to others.

The impressions we make on people have a direct effect on how we are treated. If we try to be something that we are not, that impression is transmitted to others. Like it or not, they will treat us according to the way we portray ourselves. We want to be respected for who we are and not who we try to be. We need to concentrate on being who we are and sending the true impression of ourselves to others.

In today's society, it may seem scary to be ourselves. The media asks us to join the crowd or be more like the next person. For example, television ads suggest that we should want to "be like Mike," referring, of course, to Michael Jordan. Cigarette ads lead men to believe that smoking adds to their character and women to believe that it increases their sex appeal, while they would have our children believe that they need to smoke to be cool like everyone else. The toy manufacturers want our kids to believe that they should have that toy because all the other children have it. My son, Devon, often feels that he has to say something his older sister said to merit the same attention. We often form our points of view based on what our parents believe. We are Republican or Democrat because our parents were, but we may know nothing of that party's history, what they believe, and what it means to be affiliated with them. We read the paper and listen to the news, shaping our thoughts, ideology, and philosophy by making others' thoughts our own. We do not learn how to formulate our own thoughts. Our politicians will not vote for the best bill, but for what is most popular with their party affiliation. Fear of ostracism from their party members prevents them from trusting their own consciences and doing the best for the people. It is easy to be someone else; the challenge in life comes from being yourself. It takes courage and commitment to stand up for ourselves, especially if that means standing out from the crowd.

We must strive and commit every day to affirming who we are, where we are going, and remaining true to ourselves. We do not have to be jealous of what other people have. We can't all do the same thing. I can't do what you do and you can't do what I do. But if we do what we know how to do and were created to do together, what a much better place this would be. Great problems are likely when we let ourselves be envious and overcome with jealousy toward others. We only hurt others and ourselves when we take on such negative characteristics. We hurt ourselves because we cannot grow spiritually, emotionally, and mentally when we are concentrating on what others have that we don't. We spend too much energy paying attention to others and neglecting what needs to be done with ourselves. If these characteristics get out of control, we will roll over anyone that is in our way, not caring who gets hurt in the process. We will start backbiting, lying, and whatever else it takes be like someone else. Joseph's brothers displayed these traits as they grew to hate Joseph and plotted his removal.

In his book *Even Eagles Need A Push*, David McNally writes about an eagle that has to nudge her offspring out of the nest high on the shelf of a rock cliff. He writes:

The eagle drew courage from an innate wisdom. Until her children discovered their wings, there was no purpose for their lives. Until they learned how to soar, they would fail to understand the privilege it was to have been born an eagle. The push was the greatest gift she had to offer. It was her supreme act of love; therefore, one by one, she pushed them. And they flew!

Like the eagle, until we dare to be ourselves and follow our own dreams, there is no real purpose for our lives. Unless we dare to go beyond that dream to make it reality, we will never really know how wonderful it is to have been born us. Until we learn how to use our unique experiences and talents as our wings and to soar above our fears and self-doubts, we will fail to understand the privilege it is to be us. We must first discover our own wings before we can use the winds of life to take flight as we were meant to. Until you learn how to soar with your own wings, you will never know how beautiful it is and what it really means to be you. It is with our own wings that we can begin to take flight above and beyond our valleys of self-doubt and fears and learn to endure the changing winds of life.

CHAPTER FOUR

THE "MEANWHILE" PERIOD

PERIOD

Endurance &
Persistence

VALLEY EXPERIENCES

"Here comes that dreamer," they said to each other. "Come now, let's kill him and throw him into one of these cisterns and say that a ferocious animal devoured him. Then we will see what comes of his dreams." His brother pulled Joseph out of the cistern and sold him . . . Meanwhile, the midianites sold Joseph in Egypt to Potiphor, one of Pharaoh's officials, the captain of the guard . . .
—Genesis 37: 28,36

AS I WRITE this chapter, it is now the end of October. The automobile payments are behind and there has been no steady income since the last day of July. There is no more money left in the bank, and we will have to check out of the extended stay hotel in the morning.

This is the predicament in which my family and I find ourselves. I left my job in Virginia and moved to Texas for what we believed to be an exciting and wonderful opportunity for us. We used a great deal of our savings to relocate and we sacrificed the security of where we were, with our friends, a secure job and family only a short distance away, for this wonderful opportunity. We arrived in Texas, a place where we had no friends or immediate family, on a Saturday and moved into corporate housing. Ten days after starting my new position in Texas, I terminated due to a gross misunderstanding. My family and I became, in a sense, homeless and jobless, far from family and friends, with no income or savings left in the bank. My wife and I toiled over the decision to remain in Texas and make a go of it or to head back to Virginia. Our decision was further complicated by the discovery that we were expecting a baby. The very difficult decision was made to go back to Virginia and vacate the wonderful opportunity that had lead us to Texas in the first place. We managed to scrape up enough money to drive both our cars thirteen hundred miles back to Virginia where we would stay in an extended stay hotel until I found a job and a place to live or until we ran out of money, whichever came first.

Tonight is our last night at the extended stay and we have located a place to live, but do not have all the money required to fully secure it. We cannot afford, at this moment, to have our household goods and furniture delivered from our storage in Texas. It is getting cold and our winter clothing is also in storage.

As I write this chapter, I am progressing through what I call my meanwhile period in my valley experiences. A valley experience refers to the experiencing of life's obstacles. The meanwhile period is a tran-

sitional time when it appears that we are not getting closer to our
dreams and, indeed, it may seem as though we are moving farther
away from them. The meanwhile period during our valley experiences
is the time when things in life do not go as we planned. Problem after
problem rains down upon our lives.

While in this meanwhile period during our valley experiences, it is
hard to see the proverbial silver lining or the light at the end of the tunnel. Our days are like nights and our nights are even darker. It appears
that tears mask our faces more than smiles and the pain in our hearts
leaves us breathless. In these times, we find it hard to envision ourselves
beyond where we are and the future seems so far off. We begin to look
at our lives with shame and our abilities with doubt. We question our
purpose in life and look at tomorrow with great dismay, only hoping
that things get better. We must remember that although we cannot see
the finish line during the meanwhile period, it is there just the same.

During this time, I am at a point in my life where I can allow my
situation and circumstances to dictate what and who I am, who I will
become, or what I think about. This is the point where most people
fail to find the internal courage to dare to dream; they can no longer
see beyond today's troubles and stay focused on their purpose in life.
They become victims of circumstance. It is important to note that this
is a transitional time, full of lessons and opportunities in the form of
obstacles. This is our chance to grow stronger and gain greater focus
on where we are going and where we should be. This is the time to
endure, remain persistent, and hold our heads up while taking advantage of the negative times and situations—turning them into positive
experiences. Joseph ran into his meanwhile period during his valley
experiences and in looking at his response and his reaction during
those times, we could gain courage and inspiration while learning a
very valuable lesson. A lesson of endurance and persistence.

Joseph was a young man with great dreams of becoming someone
great and doing something spectacular. He was excited about and
inspired by his great dreams. One day, however, it appeared that his
dreams were taken away from him by the terrible circumstances in his life.

Joseph's brothers were attending the flocks away from home. His
father told Joseph to go make sure all was well with his brothers and the
flocks, then return to inform him of how they were doing. When
Joseph's brothers saw him approaching, they said among themselves,

here comes that dreamer, let's kill him and then see what will come of his dreams. It was then that they decided to kill him out of envy and hatred. Reuben, Joseph's oldest brother, stood up for Joseph, suggesting that they not kill him, but throw him into the hole. Once Joseph got close enough, his brothers stripped him of the robe that his father had given him and threw him in the hole. They sat down to eat, continuing their plot of Joseph's demise and how to rid him of all his dreams.

It wasn't long before they saw a caravan of Ishmaelites (Midianites) on their way to Egypt. They concluded that rather than kill Joseph, their own flesh and blood, they would sell him to the Ishmaelites. Reuben was distraught that they had done this thing to their brother and they all devised a plan to tell their father. They killed a goat and splattered the blood on Joseph's robe, planning to tell their father that a ferocious animal devoured Joseph.

What happened to Joseph's big dreams after being sold by his own brothers into slavery? The Bible concludes the chapter with these very important words: "Meanwhile, the Midianites sold Joseph in Egypt to Potiphar, one of Pharaoh's officials, the captain of the guard." If we look closely, the New International version of the Bible concludes this chapter with the word "meanwhile." This is exciting because it suggests that something else is occurring while Joseph is being sold, his dreams being dashed. Meanwhile, a transitional phrase, suggests that we have not heard the last of this story yet. Meanwhile suggests that there is more going on than we can see with our eyes. Meanwhile suggests that all hope is not gone; there is a silver lining and there is light at the end of the tunnel. Meanwhile suggests that we not walk away, defeated with our heads down and no hope for tomorrow. Something else, unseen by the naked eye, is happening in our lives. We are being molded and shaped and put into position to go the next mile and to the next level.

Joseph had a dream, but his brothers sold him into slavery, and he was then sold again by those that bought him; meanwhile, his climb to his dreams were just starting. Meanwhile, his life is being altered to place him in the position to reach his dreams. Meanwhile, he is going through the valley of despair in order to reach the mountain of success.

The story goes on to tell us that after Joseph is sold to Potiphar, he becomes Potiphar's most trusted attendant. He is placed in charge of all that Potiphar owned. It seemed that things were looking up for Joseph. As we later learn, while Potiphar was away, his wife came to

Joseph and wanted to sleep with him, but Joseph, being that upstanding and trustworthy man that he was, would not hear of it. She tried and she tried, but Joseph would not give in. Once Potiphar returned, she told him that Joseph had tried to be with her, but she screamed and he ran out. Potiphar became angry and he had Joseph thrown into the prison—the prison where the king's prisoners were kept.

Joseph was now at a point where he could start questioning himself and his dreams. Imagine what Joseph could have been thinking about this time: "What was I thinking? How could I, a farm boy, ever think that I could become a great ruler? Look at me, locked away in prison with no hope of getting out." For sharing his sense of excitement about dreams for his future, his own flesh and blood sells him into slavery. When he is sold to Potiphar's house, he is accused of rape and imprisoned. That was not part of the dream! Where does this nightmare fit into God's glorious future for Joseph? The Bible does not record any such thing. On the contrary, once he got to prison and the warden recognized something special about him, Joseph was placed in a position over all the prisoners.

You see, when the "meanwhile" was introduced during Joseph's valley experience, it declared that what he was going through was only a transition to get him to where he should be. Meanwhile, he was being positioned to take hold of his dreams. Think about this for a moment. He had a dream that one day he would become a great ruler, but that could not happen while he was still in his father's house. Joseph's brothers may have sold him out of spite, but it was for his ultimate good. When he was sold into Potiphar's house, he was getting nearer to the throne and closer to his dream without even knowing it. If he was not sold by his brothers, then sold in Egypt to an official of the king and placed in the king's prison, he would not have obtained his dream.

Like Joseph's ordeal, our hardships may not be right or fair, but it is likely that they are readying us to achieve our dreams and to live out our purpose in life. It is important for us to understand that how we respond or react in our meanwhile period, while going through our valley experiences, will affect how long we stay in the valley and how close we will be in fulfilling our purpose in life when we come through the valley. If we examine Joseph's responses, we will see that he always did his best, no matter what the circumstances surrounding him. He never allowed his situation to rule him out; he used it to become all that he could be. Each time he was faced with obstacles, he chose to respond with positive actions and to rise to be his best.

Now, back to my situation. We have big dreams, but no money, no income, and no place to live. When "meanwhile" is introduced into my life during my valley experience, it tells me that I may not be able to see the outcome of what I am going through. Regardless, I should hold on to my dreams and not let go; there is a bright side to this darkness. I am encouraged and inspired to know that these circumstances are not my future, but can be used to get me to where I need to be.

How do I know that a "meanwhile" statement has been introduced into my life during these times? Simple—I'm so far from the finish line that I can't see it yet. Still, I will continue to run the race, I will continue to walk through this valley, and I will continue to hold on to my dream and my purpose in life. I am without money, without a home, and without a job, but you are now reading my book because of the way I responded. You now have in your hands my fulfilled dream, in spite of what I had to go through. Those things just made me stronger in the areas I needed to work on. They developed my perseverance to help me endure those times, or the meanwhile period during my valley experiences, without giving up. Meanwhile is just a transition to get us to where we need to be, and the valleys equip us with what we need to get there while we are going through. The valleys are those times in our lives when obstacles arise to make us stronger, not to break us down. Again, what we do and how we respond is very important during this meanwhile period in our valley experiences. Later in this chapter, we will discuss how to get through the valley experiences during the meanwhile period. Listen as the Apostle Paul speaks about the value of our valley experiences during the meanwhile period.

> *"…And we rejoice in the hope of the glory of God.*
> *Not only so, but we also rejoice in our sufferings,*
> *Because we know suffering produces perseverance;*
> *Perseverance, character; and character, hope.*
> *And hope does not disappoint us, because*
> *God has poured out his love into our hearts*
> *By the Holy Spirit, whom he has given us."*
>
> —Romans 5:2-5

The King James version of the Bible uses slightly different words. In short, it says that we rejoice in tribulation, which works patience, which works experience, which works hope. Another scripture has the same meaning:

> *Consider it pure joy, my brothers,*
> *whenever you face trials of many kinds,*
> *because you know that the testing of your faith*
> *develops perseverance.*
>
> —James 1:2,3

The writers of these passages are telling us that we will experience difficulties and hard times that will build us up and help us grow. To glory in our tribulation means to rejoice in suffering. We rejoice in suffering not because we enjoy pain or the tragedy of it, but because we know God is using life's difficulties to help build our character and experiences; we know that we are growing because of these things. To rejoice is merely to understand the ultimate result of our situation and not to look at our current situation as the final result. In the end, we will be better off for having gone through certain things. Problems and obstacles will develop our patience, which in turn will strengthen our character, deepen our trust in God, and give us a greater confidence in ourselves and our purpose.

You probably find your patience tested in some way every day. We should be grateful for these opportunities to grow and learn to cope. This is where we come to understand and accept our humanity and our imperfections. The ups and downs of our lives have made us who we are today, and we should learn to accept ourselves with the ups and down, the good and the bad, because they are equipping us for our unique purpose in life.

We should learn to turn the negatives into positive experiences for reaching our goals. We can do this by viewing their results as tools that will help us, rather than focusing so much on how we feel during the present trails. The result will be positive and help us grow in some way. These turbulent times help us build up the areas where we are weak, and they will help us get through the upcoming bad times with greater confidence and determination.

It would be great if we could control everything around us and all that happens in our lives. That kind of thinking is unrealistic and invariably leads to greater frustration, pain, despair and failure. We develop a resistance to events in our lives that are beyond our control and, in our minds, unfair. As the adage states, the key is to accept those things we cannot control, change the things that are within our control, know the difference, and learn from both. It's beneficial to face the predictable and the unpredictable head on.

To further illustrate my point about never giving up and always doing our best even when we do not fully understand why certain things happen to us—I am reminded of a story called "Pushing Against a Rock":

A man was asleep one night in his cabin when suddenly his room was filled with light and the Savior appeared. The Lord told the man he had work for him to do and showed him a large rock in front of the cabin. The Lord explained that the man was to push against the rock with all his might. The man did, day after day. For many years he toiled from sun up to sundown, his shoulders set squarely against the cold, massive surface of the unmoving rock, pushing with all his might. Each night, the man returned to his cabin sore and worn out, feeling that his whole day had been spent in vain.

Seeing that the man was showing signs of discouragement, Satan decided to enter the picture, placing thoughts into the man's mind: "You have been pushing against that rock for a long time and it hasn't budged. Why kill yourself over this? You are never going to move it." He was giving the man the impression that the task was impossible and that he was a failure. These thoughts discouraged and disheartened the man even more. "Why kill myself over this?" he thought. "I'll just put in my time, giving just the minimum of effort, and that will be good enough."

One day, he decided to make it a matter of prayer and take his troubled thoughts to the Lord. "Lord," he said, "I have labored long and hard in your service, putting all of my strength into that which you have asked. Yet, after all this time, I have not even budged that rock half a millimeter. What is wrong? Why am I failing?"

To this, the Lord responded compassionately, "My friend, when long ago I asked you to serve me and you accepted, I told you that your task was to push against the rock with all of your strength, which you have done. Never once did

I mention to you that I expected you to move it. Your task was to push. And now you come to me, your strength spent, thinking that you have failed. But is that really so? Look at yourself. Your arms are strong and muscled, your back strong and brown, your hands are callused from constant pressure, and your legs have become massive and hard. Through opposition, you have grown much and your abilities now surpass those that you used to have. Yet, you haven't moved the rock. But your calling was to be obedient and to push, exercising your faith and trust in my wisdom. This you have done. I, my friend, will now move the rock."

—Author Unknown

We do not know all the answers to why things happen to us, but it is important to know, understand, and accept that these things are working to help rather than hurt us. It is through the opposition, that we will grow and our abilities will surpass those that we used to have. It may not feel like it at the time, but they are there to make us stronger. Think about the tragedies that have occurred in your life and the not so pleasant encounters you have had. You may not have understood why those things were happening, but when you got through them, you were better off than when you went in. Perhaps you became stronger in your faith, gained a new sense of determination, or your patience increased. In any event, you were not the same after having gone through those trials. Of course, we also experience negative things or situations because of bad choices or decisions. We can control and minimize these things simply by making better decisions in life. Once the bad decision is made, it is very important to learn from it and walk away with a sense of growth and a greater insight to what you must do to not let this happen again.

Two instances and turning points in my life made me examine where I was in my life, giving me a new sense of motivation and urgency to reach my goals: when I lost my grandmother, who was so dear to me, and then, several years later, my father. In my mind, they were entirely too young to die and I thought it unfair that they did. Grief had stricken my heart and my mind was in a state of confusion. I could not see what good could come out of their deaths, but as I began to overcome the grief and pain, I began to realize, more than ever, that tomorrow is guaranteed to no one. I began to gain courage and strength to start living my life to the fullest each day that I have the opportunity to live. I don't know why they had to die, but I do know that I am much more aware of my mortality, the uncertainty of tomorrow, and the importance of today than ever before.

Look back over your life and take note of the tragedies and negative things that you have had to go through. Pay special attention to how you have grown mentally, physically, or spiritually because of those times. Look for the positives that were born out of the negatives—what you have learned and what is now possible because of your unique experiences in life.

I have had financial problems that have taught me to better manage my money. I have had relationship problems that helped me to better appreciate the person I am with and to take note of the things I did not want in my new relationship. I have shared personal information with those I thought were my friends and learned the valuable lesson that you cannot tell everyone everything; all who proclaim to be your friends are not always who they say they are. It is similar to children who learn by trial and error. You tell them that fire is hot and that it burns, but they still test the theory themselves, finding out that fire does burn and that burns hurt. During the process, they could only think about the pain, but once the pain ended, they became smarter, never willingly touching fire again.

Again, it is important to look for and take mental note of the lessons and positive experiences that come through the negative experiences. You will only walk away with what you want to walk away with. Too many fail to look for the positive in the negative and only take away a negative experience instead of observing the positives in each obstacle. Once we learn to look for the positive and take advantage of the lessons learned through the negative, we are more inclined to hold on to our dreams no matter what is going on in our lives. We will learn to view these things as resources to help us obtain our goals in life. We will discuss this more in another chapter.

There is another very good story, "Things Aren't Always What They Seem," that helps illustrate my point:

Two traveling angels stopped to spend the night in the home of a wealthy family. The family was rude and refused to let the angels stay in the mansion's guest room. Instead, the angels were given a small space in the cold basement. As they made their bed on the hard floor, the older angel saw a hole in the wall and repaired it. When the younger angel asked why, the older angel replied, "Things aren't always what they seem."

The next night, the pair came to rest at the house of a poor, but very hospitable farmer and his wife. After sharing what little food they had, the couple let the angels sleep in their bed where they could have a good night's rest. When the sun came up the next morning, the angels found the farmer and his wife in tears. Their only cow, whose milk had been their sole income, lay dead in the field.

The younger angel was infuriated and asked the older angel, "How could you have let this happen? The first man had everything, yet you helped him. The second family had little, but was willing to share everything, and you let the cow die."

"Things aren't always what they seem," the older angel replied. "When we stayed in the basement of the mansion, I noticed there was gold stored in that hole in the wall. Since the owner was so obsessed with greed and unwilling to share his good fortune, I sealed the wall so he wouldn't find it. Then, last night as we slept in the farmers bed, the angel of death came for his wife. I gave him the cow instead. Things aren't always what they seem."

—Author Unknown

When they occur, we may not always know why, but it is important to believe that these things happen to add to the richness of our lives, rather than to take away from us.

If we were to ask those whose names are written in our history books and those that we consider great men and women of our times what has made them great, one common thread in their answers would be that they learned from their mistakes, that problems and failures made them strong. Look over history and note the great obstacles that those who shaped America had to endure in order to reach their dream and live out their purpose. The multi-talented and, to me, the best basketball player of all time, Michael Jordan had a television commercial in which he was walking to his dressing room. We hear his voice speaking about why he is so great and he concludes it's because of all his failures. In other words, success is born from life's failures, mistakes, and troubles. We should be motivated and determined by our failures and problems not to repeat our mistakes and failures and to learn from them.

Listen to Langston Hughes as he inspires people to go for their dreams in "A Montage of Dreams Deferred":

> *Hold fast to your dreams*
> *For if dreams die,*
> *They are like a broken winged bird*
> *That cannot fly.*
> *Hold fast to your dreams*
> *For if dreams go,*
> *They are like a barren field*
> *Frozen with snow.*

This is your dream, nobody else's. Nobody can live your dream or make your dream a reality, but they can surely try to steal it away from you. The biggest thief of our dreams are ourselves. We will listen to the negative things and hang around the negative people. If we want to own a business, we listen and focus our attention on all of the reason why businesses fail, but we seldom listen and focus our attention on all the reasons why businesses succeed. We do this because we get so caught up in failure and negativity that we stop realizing that this is our dream and only we have what it takes on the inside to make it a reality. It must be inherent in you to believe that you can achieve it no matter what the obstacle. The old saying is still true: "What your mind perceives, you can achieve." Hold fast to that dream and do not allow anything or anyone, even yourself, to steal it away. Likewise, you can't make anyone else's dream come true any more than someone else can make your dream come true.

Getting back to the valley experiences, how can we get through them during the meanwhile period? I believe that the story of Joseph establishes a good solid example as to how we should respond and what we should do while going through these times. I solicited additional help on this topic from King David. I believe that there is no better example of how to get through these troubled times filled with obstacles than that found in Psalms 23, written by King David. The 23rd Psalm, as recorded by David with regard to what he had to go through and endure, provides very clear instructions and wonderful insight about getting through our valley experiences during our meanwhile period.

I once heard a cassette tape on which a preacher discussed verse four of this very same Psalm. I was so impressed by his teachings that I set out to study this text more closely and, in later years, taught on a very similar topic from the same text. I wish I knew exactly who that preacher was so that I could give him credit for helping me bring out my next few points. That preacher, whoever he was, helped me see beyond the traditional teachings of the 23rd Psalm—it also provides comforting thoughts and words during times of turmoil in order to extract the answers for enduring our negative life experiences. That preacher made several key points in his sermon regarding the fourth verse of the 23rd psalm and how we get through our difficult times. He made it clear that when we are going through negative situations in our lives, we should acknowledge the realism of our problems, acknowledging that they exist. We should then announce our response during these times—what we are going to do about our problems. Then we should call on our resource during these times; we should know what we have in God and have been given by God to help us through. It was not until I started to write this chapter that I remembered that sermon and began to study this magnificent Psalm more closely. The more I studied this Psalm and the life of King David, the more I became convinced of the preacher's conclusions and the answers they provided me for getting through our valley experiences. I believe that you, too, will see the value of the 23rd Psalm and what it brings to us as we go through our valley experiences. We will take a moment to focus on the three points mentioned above, taken from the fourth verse of the 23rd Psalm.

Before I get to those three main points, Allow me a brief moment to expand on the story of King David and what inspired him to write the 23rd Psalm. In my opinion, the 23rd Psalm has motivated and inspired many people, both Christians and non-Christians. The Psalm was inspired by God and put to paper by King David, who, at the time of its writing, was a man in great trouble and serious turmoil. His very life was in grave jeopardy at this time. He was running for his life and found himself in a valley experience during his meanwhile period. The Psalm, that King David wrote, is about people just like us who have been or are currently in their valley experience during their meanwhile period, pressing to grab hold of their purpose in life. It is for people who may be at the brink of giving up on their dreams, people who need to know that there is a bright side to this dark night, and people who need to be comforted. It lets us know that we are not alone and, most importantly, it confirms that we can make it through these troubled times.

Most of us remember King David as the great king, the ruler chosen by God to lead and rule over his people of Israel and as the great slayer of the giant Goliath. He was a man with so much hope and promise. Like Joseph, King David was to become a great king, but before he ascended the throne and after being declared king of the throne, he had to go through his valley experiences during his meanwhile period. God had ordained King David, even in his youth, through his prophet Samuel.

It is important to note that David was a very unlikely candidate to be the next king of Israel. He had brothers that were strong, well-built men and better looked the part. Nevertheless, God says to Samuel, as he is looking for the right person to bless and eventually become king, "I do not look at what man looks like; it is not the outside appearance, but the heart that I look at." David is recorded as being handsome and ruddy, but even with his fine appearance, he hardly looked how a king was expected to look. People looked up to kings that had a bold and strong appearance, but this David was ruddy. It was necessary to look beyond outward appearances and shortcomings and see the possibilities of what he could become.

In the same way, others may count us out of the race and view our dreams as ridiculous because of how they see us. There is one great flaw with that kind of thinking; they do not know what we have on the inside that can make us great. Others often judge our capabilities by our outward appearance. If we are not careful, we will fall into the trap of believing what others think about us and the limitations they place on us because of what they see. Let us remember that they only have a piece of the whole story because they can only see the outside, but we know there is a whole lot more to us than what they see. It is important to remember the farm boy, Joseph, who went on to become a great leader and this ruddy David who went on to not only become a great king, but an extremely effective and powerful warrior and military leader. In a subsequent chapter, we will continue to discuss the way we view ourselves.

The unlikely future ruler of Israel, David later slays Goliath and is asked to serve in the king's service. As David's popularity grew, so did King Saul's jealousy of him. It grows so strong that he tries on several occasions to kill David. In order to avoid being caught, David was forced to spend a great deal of time hiding and running for his life. Saul could see David's greatness and ability to be the next king, but could not tolerate the thought of someone else being greater than he. This may sound strikingly similar to our own lives. When we have big dreams and start living out our purpose in life, not everyone is going to be happy for us or take our side. Just like us, David had to endure great hardship and persevere through life-threatening situations before reaching his destiny—the throne. In other words, he was running into obstacles in his valley experiences during his meanwhile period, the period between getting to and actually achieving his destiny.

Once David ascends the throne, he still has obstacles that he must overcome if he is to continue to live out his purpose in life. One of his greatest challenges was his son's conspiracy against him to take over the throne. When King David's own son set out to kill him, David again ran for his life and went into exile. Eventually, after much hardship and adversity, King David regained control of the throne. Through the 23rd Psalm, we note that even with all David's negative experiences, he still held on to what he knew was his purpose in life. His unique experiences helped him carry out his purpose in life.

Sometime during or after all this, he sat down to write the 23rd Psalm. Some believe he wrote it when running for his life from King Saul. Others believe it was while he was running from his own son who wanted to kill him and overthrow him as king. No matter when it was, he left a great example of what our response to adversity should be and how we should go through our valley experiences during our meanwhile period. His words give us the courage to face the obstacles that prevent us from going where we should. They help us during that period of time when things seem to be standing still or going backward, when it appears we are making no forward progress in life.

The Lord is my shepherd; I shall not want. He maketh me to lie down in green pastures: He leadeth me beside the still waters. He restoreth my soul: He leadeth me in the paths of righteousness for his name's sake. Yea though I walk through the valley of the shadow of death, I will fear no evil: for thou art with me; thy rod and thy staff they comfort me. Thou preparest a table before me in the presence of mine enemies: thou anointest my head with oil; my cup runneth over. Surely goodness and mercy shall follow me all the days of my life: And I will dwell in the house of the Lord for ever.

—Psalm 23 (KJV)

In verse four of this 23rd Psalm, David provides some key ingredients for getting through our valley experiences during our meanwhile period. "Yea (even) though I walk through the valley of the shadow of death, I will fear no evil for thou art with me. Thy rod and thy staff they comfort me." David says that if we are to get through our valley experiences, we must first be willing to acknowledge the reality of the valley. This means that we must first admit to ourselves that there is something wrong, that there is an obstacle to overcome, or that we are going through some rough times. You see, the reason that many of us do not get through our valley experiences, or get over and beyond our problems or obstacles by spending time working on them, is because we do not admit that there is actually a problem. It is not that we do not see the problem or obstacle in our way, but we sometimes believe that if we ignore it, it will go away or if we do not acknowledge it, no one else will see it. It is hard to get over, beyond, or out of something that you claim is not there or take up a good fight against something that you claim you do not see.

In other words, if the alcoholic is to be successful and achieve his goal of no longer drinking, he must first admit that he is an alcoholic or that he has a problem. If the liar is to stop lying and the drug abuser is to break his habit, they must first admit that they have a problem. The same applies if a physically abused wife continues denying that both her husband and their relationship have a problem; she will continue to be abused and their relationship will continue to suffer. The same principle holds true in relation to other situations in which we find ourselves—from finances to relationships to our work. We will continue to have problems with our finances if we pretend that we have a handle on them when, in reality, we have no idea where all our money has gone by the end of the month. Our relationships will continue to sour if, rather than dealing with the problem, we pretend that we are not having problems or that things will improve with time. In order to pull out of these negative situations and move on with our lives, we must acknowledge that they exist. We must not deny that there are or will be obstacles in our lives; we can't just pretend that they are not there when we run into them. We have to take the good with the bad. If we are to improve the bad or turn the bad into the positive, we first must admit to ourselves that there is a problem.

The psalmist acknowledges in verse four that he was in the valley and that he knows he will have to endure unpleasant things in his life. "Shadow of death" may not mean imminent death or grave danger exclusively, but also the acknowledgment and recognition of obstacles always present in valley experiences. It is a valley we cannot go around, over, or under; we just have to go through it. Now that the valley experiences have been acknowledged, one can devise a plan to get through and beyond them. Acknowledging that there is a problem, situation, or obstacle in our lives is like laying out a roadmap. Once we get to that point, we are then able to chart the next point on our map. If we bypass points in the road, we cannot hope to get to our destination; we will only get lost.

David first acknowledged the reality of his valley experience. We must realize that the valley or the bad things that happen to us are just as much a part of our lives as breathing. Whether we are big or strong, rich or poor, Protestant or Catholic, we all have to go through our valley experiences. What we do when faced with these valley experiences will greatly depend on how and when we come through. If we understand that bad things really do happen to good people, that they are not meant to destroy us, but to help us grow, then we are able to affirm in our minds and hearts that we can handle them no matter what.

It is important to note what the psalmist is actually doing in the fourth verse of the 23rd Psalm. He is walking. The verse "Yea though I walk through the valley . . . ." is important. The mere fact that he is walking during his most troublesome time in life, while going through his valley experiences, tells me that he understands exactly what a valley is. He understands that his problems are only temporary, that they will not last forever. He knows that if he keeps on walking and moving forward, he will get through his valley. A valley is merely a depression between two hills; therefore, if he keeps on walking, he will eventually reach the other side. When we do not understand this truth about the valley, we either become lost, losing focus during our roughest times, or we prolong our misery. We become overwhelmed or "make a mountain out of a mole hill," so to speak. When this happens, we find our-selves sitting down in the valley; if we sit too long, we will end up home-steading in the valley. When we give up, when we make more out of our situation than it really is, and when we become so overwhelmed by our situation that we lose all hope and buckle under the weight of despair, we begin to see no way out. We are only prolonging our stay in the negative situation or our valley. Again, we must recognize that it is only a valley, a depression between two hills, and that we are going to get through it if we don't stop walking, if we don't lose focus, and if we don't give up hope.

In addition, when we are going through our valley experiences, we must announce our response. Listen to what King David said when he was going through his valley experiences: "Yea though I walk through the valley of the shadow of death, I will fear no evil for thou are with me. Thy rod and thy staff they comfort me." If we are going to get through our valley experiences during our meanwhile period, it is important for us to first acknowledge that there is a problem or obsta-cle, a valley. Once we have done that, we are able to announce what we are going to do next, our response to our valley experiences. How we respond when we go through something directly affects how long we stay in that situation and how we will come through that situation. King David says, "Yes, I am in trouble and, yes, death may be following in my shadows, but I will fear no evil." While he acknowledges that it will be frightening to persevere, he knows that he has to go through these things to achieve the results. He will not give up. To announce your response to your valley experiences does not mean that you will not be scared, it does not mean that you do not have some apprehension or doubt. It simply makes it known that you are not alone and what you can do in God and with God. It announces that you have what it takes on the inside to overcome any obstacle or situation and that you real-ize that these things will only make you stronger in the end.

It is noteworthy to mention that there is a difference between responding and reacting so that we do not confuse the two and end up reacting to a problem instead of responding to it. According to *Webster's Dictionary*, react means to respond to a stimulus, to be affected by some influence; a reaction to a return or opposing action, force, influence, or response to a stimulus or influence. A response, however, is something said or done in answer, reply, or reaction, to have a positive or favorable reaction. Therefore, a reaction is what or how we respond as a consequence of what happens to us. In other words, our reaction is a response influenced or stimulated by our situation and is often based on our feelings and emotions. Conversely, a response is providing a positive reaction or reply to our situation instead of allowing our situation to build or create our reaction for us. Our response is our answer and affirmation that we give when we are confident in our innate ability to get through any given situation and the faith we have in a power beyond ourselves. When we only react as things happen to us, people can manipulate us, because they know that when they do certain things to us, we will react in a certain way. But when we are confident in what God has planted on the inside of us as well as our abilities and purpose in life, we will respond in a way that will announce that we will not give up or give in to the situation.

We find David saying that no matter what is going on around him, he will not stop, sit down, or pause, but that he will continue to walk without fear, because he knows that the only way to get through is to keep walking without getting distracted or overwhelmed by the situation. Of course, there are things in our lives that we would like to change and that we would change if we could, but since we can't, we are going to have to walk through the valley. Announce your response: "I will walk through my valley." Know that you have what it takes on the inside to get you through.

The last point is that we must learn to use our resources while we go through our valley experiences. It is not enough to acknowledge that you are faced with a bad situation, or your valley experience, and then determine that you will walk through. We have to learn to use our resources while we are going through these tough times. We must remember that God is walking with us through these times. In the fourth verse, David says, "I will fear no evil for though art with me, thy rod and thy staff, they comfort me." In addition, the 23rd Psalm starts with and ends with God. God is walking with you and God is in the valley with you. David is not afraid because he knows who and what his resources are. He understands that God is with him, that he has what it takes on the inside, and knows that the outcome will far exceed his present situation. That is the silver lining, the light at the end of the tunnel—what we will gain once we get through our valley experiences during our meanwhile period.

We should be encouraged during our meanwhile periods, because when we understand that the pursuit of our dreams are not without these times, we then become determined to move ahead in spite of the obstacles. These valleys during our meanwhile period comes to all of us, but we must understand and be encouraged by the fact that they are a part of life and are instrumental in our growth, achievement, and success. Those that fail to understand that will find themselves trapped by their own limitations and fears.

Life's situations can become so bad that we lose focus of our goals and are ready to give up, but I believe that we take the first steps to achieving our dreams through making them known, by acknowledging that that this will not be easy, but we can handle it and will go forward. Positive thinking begins to happen and resources to help us achieve and get through these times begin to appear; from out of nowhere, we find encouragement to press on rather than giving up. When we make the commitment to move, then everything around us moves in harmony with us to meet our needs and achieve our goals. Without our first actions, the "how" it will be accomplished may never be answered. The commitment of the first step toward our dreams has more power than we may believe.

Everyone faces these valley experiences during their meanwhile period, better known as life's obstacles and adversity. This is the period in time where we appear to be standing still, going nowhere, or moving backward. The key to how we will come through these times will be what we do during this period. Will we maintain a positive attitude or will we just give up? Will we make excuses or look for the silver lining? Will we be one of the majority and just complain about our situation or will we use our situations as stepping stones of opportunity to climb closer to our goals?

Never lose focus of your dream, your purpose in life, no matter what happens or what goes on around you. It will ultimately be our willingness to stay focused, be persistent, and hold on to our goals that will lead to our success. Our present situations are an opportunity to be the best that we are, where we are, until we get to where we want to be. Therefore, no matter how difficult the situation or how rough the road we travel, we are never defeated or lost as long as we remain focused. As Paul writes in II Corinthians 4:8,9:

> *We are troubled on every side, yet not distressed;*
> *we are perplexed, but not in despair;*
> *Persecuted, but not forsaken;*
> *cast down, but not destroyed . . .*

Paul's words remind us that though we may be at the end of our rope, we are never at the end of hope. As he was living out his life's purpose, he faced sufferings, trials, and distress, but he knew that they would end one day and he would obtain his reward. As we face great troubles, it's easy to focus on the pain rather than on our ultimate goal. Just as athletes concentrate on the finish line and ignore their discomfort, we must focus on the result that will come through our belief in ourselves and our faith and perseverance. It is easy to give up and quit. We all have faced problems in our homes, relationships, or work that caused us to want to lay down the tools in our hands and walk away. Don't grow weary or let the pain, defeats, or criticism force you to lose your focus and stray off the path. Life's troubles should not diminish our belief in our faith or set limits on us. We should realize that there is a purpose in our suffering. Our ultimate hope in terrible illness, persecution, or pain is realizing that this period in our lives is not all there is. There is life after the valley!

We are subjected to every kind of human weakness, persecution, and suffering. However, the future, in all its' glorious uncertainty, eclipses any suffering the present can hold. We can still persevere and keep our heads above water. Whatever condition or "meanwhile" we may have introduced into our life simply means that there is more to our lives than we may be able to see and that there is more going on than the troubles we may be experiencing today.

As written in Paul's passage in II Corinthians, there is a "but not" statement introduced into our lives, which keeps us from losing heart and comforts us with the faith and belief in tomorrow. We may find ourselves in bad shape, but never truly defeated. We may find ourselves troubled on every side, yet not distressed; we may be perplexed, but not in despair; we may be persecuted, but not forsaken; we may be cast down, but not destroyed. This is true even during the middle of our valley experiences in our meanwhile period.

CHAPTER FIVE

"I AM," NOT "THEY ARE"

Responsibility

You intended to harm me, but God intended it for good to accomplish what is now being done, the saving of many lives . . .
                                                    —Genesis 50:19-21

IT'S NOT MY fault...If my parents would have...If the blacks will start...If the whites will stop...If I grew up in a better...Teachers are not doing...The government is not doing...The politicians are not...If only they would have...Then I could or would have...and the Devil made me do it.

We live in a time where we see and hear people blame everyone but themselves for where they are and then use that as an excuse not to move ahead or dream. They hold everyone else responsible for their lives. This mentality gives others more power over our lives than they should rightfully possess. We have seen it and perhaps, at one time or another, done it ourselves: passing the buck, pointing the finger, scapegoating. So it was with Adam and Eve blaming each other for their own dismiss, it continues today. We will use our own negative situations and what has been done to us as excuses to do nothing at all or to do wrong ourselves. Society has, in turn, given us many excuses for not holding ourselves accountable for our current situation. Those excuses are even given names, thereby validating them. Society blames "road rage" for people running one another off the road. Insanity pleas oftentimes free murderers from prison or decrease their sentences. Suppressed memory syndrome, say psychologists, explains why people are the way they are. Then there are those that blame the unfair treatment of their ancestors for their current predicaments, stating that they cannot progress like the other nationalities or races. Please do not misunderstand: I do believe that the above conditions exist and possibly play a role in some situations, but in the end, people must take full responsibility for themselves and their actions if they are going to take control of their lives and live out their purpose.

The warning label on a pack of cigarettes warns that smoking can be hazardous to your health, but millions of people continue to smoke. Millions have become deathly ill because of their long-term habit of smoking, yet they point fingers and successfully sue cigarette manufacturers for their illnesses.

Drugs have taken many lives in one way or another, even with the "Just Say No" campaign in the schools, homes, and media. Naturally, we blame drugs for shootings and resultant deaths, not realizing that it is the actual demand of the drugs that keeps them coming and that that demand is coming from individuals who are making the choice to use drugs.

Millions of people have become shooting victims, yet we have mounted a defense of those pulling the trigger by blaming it on the availability of guns and going after those who make guns. Perhaps we should worry more about the troubled mind that pulled the trigger. We blame our children's music for the horrific crimes or acts they commit rather than focusing on the disturbing thought of what attracted them to the music and made them act on these thoughts.

The Bible says that it is not what goes into a man that makes him unclean, but what comes out of a man that makes him unclean. This is not to say that we should not monitor what we listen to, who we choose to be around, and which advice we accept, but it does warn us that we are responsible for what ultimately comes out of us. We are responsible for what we say, what we do, and the decisions we make. While it is important, then, to be careful what we take in if it influences what we put out, we are accountable in the end.

Prior to joining the Navy, I took the exam to go into the Air Force and received a very good score. I signed up for the U.S. Air Force that same day. When the time came for me to leave for the Air Force military processing station and continue on to basic training, family members drove me to the bus station. When I said goodbye to my grandmother, I saw in her eyes how proud she was of her grandson, now going off to the Air Force to make something of himself. I, too, was full of great dreams and high hopes for myself. I would get my college degree and be the best military person that anyone had ever seen.

At the processing station, I signed lots of papers and was finally sworn into the Air Force. However, one final procedure remained before heading off to basic training. I sat with the staff sergeant who would go over all my paperwork and ensure that every thing was complete. I was asked if I had ever used drugs. I thought for a moment and said that yes, I had experimented with drugs not long ago at a gathering back home. Marijuana was being passed around and I, feeling the pressure from those around me, inhaled once and passed it on. I felt no harm in telling that truth.

The staff sergeant looked at me as if not believing what he had just heard. He pulled a piece of paper from a pile and showed it to me.

The piece of paper was a signed document by me, stating that I had never used drugs before. He asked if that was my signature and if I remembered signing that document. The answer to both was yes. He then said, "Because of what you admitted to me and what you have signed, I am going to have to discharge you from the Air Force." I was stunned, dismayed, confused, angry, disappointed, and scared. I was furious with the staff sergeant; I had been honest with him and could not believe his nerve. I thought he was wrong for doing this to me and could not believe that the government would let him get away with it. I was a good person, hard worker, received good grades, and everyone liked me. This could not be happening.

He proceeded to discharge me and got me tickets for the bus back home. In addition to my anger, I began to wonder what my grandmother would think. What would my mother and father say and what would be the reaction of my friends back home when they saw that I had failed? Still believing that the staff sergeant was to blame, I got to the bus station, called my congressman, and told his staff the story. They, too, could not believe it, at least the way that I told the story, and said that the congressman wanted me to stay where I was while he looked into it. I was sure now that the staff sergeant would get what was coming to him and that I would not have to make that call home. The pay phone rang and the congressman on the other end told me there was nothing he could do because of the Air Force policy on drugs, but he wanted to make sure I got back home. Now dejected, angry, my dreams crushed, and still scared, I called home and told my grandmother the story. That was one of the longest bus rides I had ever taken.

Once I returned home, I could see that my grandmother blamed herself and this hurt even more because of my great love for her. Now, I could have spent my time blaming the staff sergeant for discharging me and the congressman for not doing enough to help me, but in doing that, I would be giving control of my future to the situation instead of controlling my future by taking responsibility for my actions. The staff sergeant may have discharged me and the congressman may not have taken the fight to a higher level, but my original actions caused the reaction of the Air Force and ultimately led to my discharge. It was a decision to remain positive and to accept responsibility for my own actions that enabled me to move forward and go after my dreams. Not one week passed before I went down to the Navy recruiter and signed on under a drug waiver. I graduated from the Navy basic training with a meritorious advancement, became the top sailor everywhere I was stationed, went on to school and graduated at the top of my class, and now you are holding my book in your hands. I could have, like many, remained in the past blaming others; instead, I chose to turn a negative situation into a positive future—by taking responsibility for my actions.

We hear horror stories of women getting so drunk that they become defenseless against men who take advantage of them. Yes, men who take advantage of them are wrong and should be punished, but at the same time, we must be held accountable and responsible for our own actions. We hear the media talk about the otherwise good person who is locked in jail for vehicular manslaughter, because he made a decision to drink and drive, running his car head-on into another and killing someone. People are behind bars because of "road rage." Their lives have been altered because of one moment of uncontrollable rage, perhaps running another car off the road when that person cut them off in traffic. There are the jealous spouses who, in the heat of the moment, stab or shoot their counterpart, and spawned ex-spouses who commit terrible acts because of pain and denial.

These individuals cannot blame the alcohol, guns, knives, or anything else but themselves for what has happened to them. Instead, if they are to take back control of their lives, they must hold themselves accountable and take responsibility for their actions. They must begin by looking inward and asking themselves what role they played in their current predicament.

Those may be extreme cases, but there are plenty of everyday cases where we hear people blame others for where they are in life instead of taking responsibility. Grown children blame their parents when they are not successful adults, claiming that Mom and Dad didn't take an active role in their lives when they were young. The husband blames his lack of success on his wife's lack of support in his endeavors. The wife claims she cannot be herself because of her husband's lack of understanding. The blacks blame the whites for holding them back and preventing them from achieving their dreams. The whites blame the blacks for monopolizing the job market and positions in schools, hindering their progress in life. The Protestants and Catholics blame each other for not teaching the way they feel they should. We blame teachers, who are underpaid and overworked in understaffed schools, for our children not doing well in school. Citizens are blaming the government for lack of concern about their issues, politicians are blaming the White House for not prioritizing the concerns of the people, and the President is blaming Congress for playing politics.

There is enough blame and finger-pointing to go around, but not enough of us taking responsibility for our own lives and actions. When it comes to our own lives and what we should be achieving, we must hold ourselves ultimately accountable for where we are and take responsibility for our decisions that brought us to our current place. We point the fingers at exterior problems instead of looking closely at the interior issues. We cannot move forward to achieve great things until we accept full responsibility for who we are, where we are, and the decisions we made that got us there.

This is not to say that we should never hold others accountable. Others may have had a very big influence on where we are and the situations or predicaments in which we find ourselves. Outside sources such as music, cigarette ads, and the availability of guns may influence, compound, or inflate issues in our lives; however, we must ultimately decide that we are responsible for where we are now and what will come next. Our choices have consequences, good and bad. The choices are ours; therefore, the consequences of those choices are also ours.

I cannot blame others for my predicaments or for not reaching a goal, because that mentality establishes limits on how far I can and will go in life. I will never move forward if I allow others to hold me back, real or imagined. It is hard to mend or strengthen weak areas in my life when I am blaming others for my issues, but as soon as I realize that I am responsible, I can begin to see where I need help, recognize what went wrong, and overcome my situation. Taking responsibility allows me to move forward to where I should be. When we take responsibility for our thoughts, actions, and decisions, we then take control of our lives and our destinies; we begin to develop our roadmap to success. Instead of moving through life upset at your parents for not being there, your friends for their peer pressure, your teachers for not getting you on the right track, or any other outside influence or contributor, it is time to ask yourself what you have done to get here. Then ask what you have done to correct the situation.

Mistakes are an unavoidable side effect of being human. We all make them and they can be important contributors to our life process.

The tragic part is when we don't learn from them. For example, if a child were caught shoplifting, he would have two choices. He could admit that he did wrong, learn from his mistake, and never do it again. However, many blame the person who caught them and society for forcing them to steal. As adults, they're likely to be found living lives of crime or locked behind bars.

Joseph was stripped of his clothes, thrown into a pit, and sold into slavery by his brothers. Once he was appointed and settled as the head of household for an important person in Egypt to whom he was sold, he was falsely accused of trying to rape the wife of his master and then thrown into jail. Once he settled into jail and became the head of the other prisoners, the people he helped in jail betrayed him. The amazing thing about this story is that he didn't complain about his situation or those that contributed to his situation. He had every right to be angry with his brothers who, because of their jealousy, wanted Joseph out of the way, so much so that they threw him into the pit and sold him into slavery. He could have very easily spent his life blaming them for his situation, but, in doing so, he would have missed the lessons and the rewards that came out of his terrible ordeal.

It would be so easy, when going though crises like Joseph's, to not only blame others for the way our lives have gone, but to give up on our hopes and dreams. Joseph could have said, "Yea, I had big dreams of becoming someone in a position of prestige and power, but now look. I am merely a slave, sold like a possession with no prestige and treated as a prisoner with no power. How can I achieve my goals and dreams when I was sold as a slave by my own brothers and locked in prison by my master? I have tried and tried; I became the head of my master's household and the head of the prison, but still I am no one and far from having power and prestige." Although these thoughts may have entered Joseph's mind, he did not show it nor does the text tell us he vocalized it. He did not sit back and spend his days blaming his brothers; instead, he took control and responsibility and maintained a positive attitude. The text may not have specifically said that he had a positive mind the entire time, but it is evident that he was always recognized as being special and very capable, thus placed in positions of leadership. Therefore, not only was God with Joseph during these times, he decided not to sink into self-pity and play the blame game. He was determined to be the best that he could be no matter where he was and what situation he was in. Rather than complaining, which he had the right to do, he accepted where he was in life and took advantage of every opportunity. He took responsibility for his own life, deciding to control the things he could and leave the things he could not control to a higher power.

At the close of this story, Joseph's dream of being a great leader became reality and he realized, after seeing his brothers again, that he had to go through what he did in order to get where he was. The amazing reality of what he went through was summed up in his words to his brothers: "You intended to harm me, but God intended it for good to accomplish what is now being done, the saving of many lives."

Although at one time he may have blamed them for what they did to him, he found that it was useless. If he had not been sold into slavery in Egypt, then he might never have become the ruler of Egypt. His brothers may have intended to destroy him, but God had other plans for his life. It is important to remember that if Joseph had fallen pray to blaming his brothers for his life, he would not have had the positive attitude to be his very best and could have lost focus of who he was to become. Blaming others would have made a tragedy of his situation; instead, he turned his situations into success.

Once we start to blame others for our lives, we give them control of our lives and our situations. By pointing fingers at others and pitying ourselves, we lose focus and deplete precious energy that could be used to realize our potential. We must be determined to do and be our very best, no matter what the situation. We can use our present situations as stepping stones or stairs to get to where we belong. This doesn't mean that we should allow others to harm us or make our lives miserable. Again, we should take control of those situations we can change and leave the rest to God. It is easy to play victim of our circumstance and envy the achievements of others rather than using what is inside us to take control of our lives. Once you have decided to accept responsibility for who and where you are, then you will be better equipped to take hold of your future.

It is vitally important in taking responsibility for our future that we take "them," "they," and "you" out of our lives and replace them with "I." It is not they that are responsible for me, or them that made me the way I am, or you who can control where I am going. I am the only one responsible for myself; I am the one that controls my actions and where I am going. Only I am responsible for me.

CHAPTER SIX

BREAKING DOWN NEGATIVE WALLS

Self-Doubt

"WHAT WE THINK ABOUT OURSELVES"

But while Joseph was there in the prison, the lord was with him . . . So the warden put Joseph in charge of all those held in the prison, and he was responsible for all that was done there. . . .

—Genesis 39: 21,22

"IT HAS BEEN seventeen years now and I have not been able to sleep at night because of anxiety pains," an elderly women told me while I was sitting in the waiting area of the Veterans Administration (VA) hospital in Maine. I had just been ordained and appointed to lead the Protestant chapel services at the naval station in Winter Harbor, Maine. The elderly woman sitting next to me saw me reading my Bible and asked if I was a preacher.

"Yes, ma'am," I replied.

She told me she had asked because something about me stood out. "May I speak with you a moment, preacher?""she asked and I was happy to talk with her.

"My husband and I have been to different doctors and we have been to my pastor about our situation. I have recently converted from Catholicism to Christianity in the Methodist church after being a Catholic all my life. I have these anxiety pains that keep me uncomfortable throughout the day, and I have been unable to sleep at night for the past seven years. My husband gets them, too, but not so bad that he can't sleep. I just want to ask you a couple of questions that I have not gotten a good answer for yet."

"Yes, ma'am, please go ahead and ask."

"I pray to God every night," she said. "I read my Bible and I do what it says the best that I can. I just need to know: Why has God not answered my prayers? Am I not praying right? Why would he not do anything when he sees that I am in such pain?" With this last question, she looked directly into my eyes and hers were filled with tears. "Is God real?"

Here I was, this new preacher and pastor, ready to take on the world and this women was asking questions that demanded answers. My answer would mean a lot to her, possibly determining whether she would continue praying and seeking God's face. I spoke with her for a little while and prayed with her and her husband, but I felt that my answer was so inadequate for what she needed.

I left that hospital feeling like a dejected fraud, as if I had let her down. I felt that I did not deserve to be a minister because I could not, at that critical moment, give an answer to the realness of the one in whom I professed my faith and taught about. This was a very pivotal point in my life. I had to make a decision as to what I would do next. I could have decided from this encounter that I was not fit to be a minister any longer and quit, or I could have used that situation to make me a better minister and to help me grow. A war raged inside of me as to what I should do, but I discovered my next step. I decided that I was not going to let this encounter deter me from doing what I knew I should be doing, but would instead use this situation as a positive learning tool. This encounter could have so easily caused me to doubt myself instead of checking my direction. It could have caused me to establish clear limits for myself as to how far I could go in life. It is bad enough to allow others to set limits on us, but it is even worse when we set limits on ourselves based on our current situation and what others think about us.

It is vital that we adopt some of Joseph's characteristics if we are to live out our purpose in life. Joseph could have easily blamed others for his predicament, giving them control of his future. As mentioned earlier, he had every reason to doubt the fulfillment of his dreams and his ability to achieve those dreams. Regardless, Joseph continued to be the very best that he could be with what he had, no matter what the situation.

When he was sold to one of the king's officials, he could have done just enough to get by or rebelled because of his situation, but he worked hard and was rewarded by being placed in charge. When he is later thrown into prison, he continues to work hard instead of complaining about his past or how he does not belong there. His hard work and determination pay off again when he is placed in a position of leadership. It did not matter where Joseph came from or what had happened to him, only how he handled the present and set himself up for the future. By not letting his past affect his future in a negative way, he was positioning himself to take hold of his dreams for the future. If he had not reacted the way he did, he could not have realized his dreams. By knocking down his walls of self-doubt and not giving up on today because of yesterday, he opened the doors of possibility for tomorrow.

In one of his recorded sermons, Reverend Freddy Haynes of Friendship West Baptist Church in Dallas, Texas speaks of a news segment that concluded with a spotlight on a vulture named Burt who was born and nurtured in captivity. They said that Burt would not fly more than ten feet above the ground because he was raised in captivity. Although Burt has the wings and the ability to fly above ten feet over the ground, he never will because of the imaginary limits he has placed on himself from being held in captivity. His physical capability is limited by his own mentality. Reverend Frederick Haynes concludes that, "In this life it is not your locality nor your personality but your mentality, when informed by your spirituality, that shapes your reality." Many of us have been in positions where our situations may have temporarily prevented us from doing all that we wanted to do or going as far as we wanted to go. Those barriers, like Burt's situation, are only temporary and once we have gotten beyond them, we are limited only by our thinking and nothing else. It has very little or nothing to do with where we are in our present life, our status, the silver spoon in our mouth, or whether we are rich or poor. It has very little or nothing to do with how likable we may or may not be, but it has a whole lot to do with our mentality and how we view ourselves. Yes, presence or the lack of things such as social status, money, or even color may make it easier or harder on us, but in the end, the final result will be a result of how badly we want it. If we allow our situations or others to place limitations on us, then we will remain forever down on the ground with the capability to soar like an eagle, achieve our goals, and live out our purpose, but also the disbelief in our own capabilities to lift off. Burt needed to be able to break down the imagery walls of captivity, as we need to break down our imagery walls of disbelief in ourselves that have been formed over time

We spend too much time thinking about and dwelling on what others think about us and all the mistakes we have made in the past. We also spend entirely too much time casting judgments on ourselves because of the mistakes we have made. Then there is the valuable time wasted when we start comparing ourselves to others who have nothing to do with where we are going or our purpose in life. These things contribute to self-doubt, which leads to self-imposed limitations and excuses as to why we can't achieve our dreams. What's important is what we think about ourselves and that we learn from our past mistakes and problems. We should realize that our past issues and experiences make us unique and are an important factor in who we are today. That uniqueness equips us to live out our purpose in life.

We must understand that those mistakes we have made, problems we have faced, and negative situations in our lives help to make us strong and provide us with valuable insight into our own thinking and our purpose if we only learn to deal with them. It is important to learn from setbacks and negative situations, but far too many of us get caught up in past experiences and are unable to move forward, thereby creating imaginary walls of self-doubt. Those walls can cripple any dream we have if we let them. If we let these things go without dealing with them, the walls become bigger and wider. We must learn how to effectively deal with our past so that we can allow it to help us toward a brighter future. In order to break down these walls, we must, as discussed in the last chapter, stand and take responsibility for them, but then we must take a hard look at where we are and where we want to go. Then we must tackle each wall individually and see how we can use it to further our progress in life.

We have to start by believing in ourselves, that we do have a purpose in life. We must believe that God will forgive us and then be willing to forgive ourselves. God created us and God has given each of us something in life to do. God accepts us as we are and we should try accepting ourselves in the same manner. Only then can we begin to make the necessary changes in our lives. This action also includes learning to forgive others and releasing the wrongs that have been committed against you. Let them go. Break down that wall. People have more power and control over us when we harbor resentment and anger toward them for the wrongs that they have done.

I want you to see that we will take chances and risks while pressing toward our goals and living out our purpose. Our right choices will be made from the bad choices, and our successes will be born from our failures—just as laughter is born out of our tears. In our weakness, we find strength; in our tears, we find hope; in our pain, we find comfort. Without one, you cannot have the other. We need to realize the value of our past mistakes and problems without allowing the past to become our present and our future.

When self-doubt begins to invade our thoughts, we pay more attention to why we should not rather than why we should, why we cannot rather than why we can, why we are unable rather than why we are able, and what we do not have rather than what we do have. With this mentality, we lose control of our lives and give it over to the naysayers and to our past problems, mistakes, situations, and judgments. These walls of self-doubt need to be broken down. These walls help give way to our own fears and doubts. We begin to adopt the negative thoughts around us as our reality and begin to focus on all the reason we cannot achieve our dreams. We begin to let our situations and everyone else set limits on how high we can go, what we can achieve, and what our destination will be. Before we know it, we have built a wall or several walls of self-doubt.

We don't break down the walls of self-doubt by running away from past negativity, but by identifying and facing it head on. We must firmly face the negative thoughts by seeing the many positives within them. Once we identify why we feel that we can't achieve something, we then dispel that thought by replacing it with why we can. This comes by realizing what factors are against us and eliminating them one at a time. We will then feel more powerful to handle any situation and see that more doors of opportunity will open. It also gives us more freedom to choose the direction of our lives and make choices that will help place us in the midst of endless possibilities. Once we stop worrying about the past by breaking down these walls, our hopes and dreams can be released into endless possibilities where only the sky is the limit.

Therefore, if we accept the negative wall of "I don't have what it takes to achieve my goal or dreams" and we look at what it actually takes to achieve our dream, we can compare the two and see what remains. Take the remainder and break it down until it is within your reach or until you have figured out an alternative. You will have then broken down that wall.

From the start, most of us accept what authority figures say about us as gospel and let it affect our own thoughts of what we can and cannot do. For example, Michael Jordan was told at a young age that he did not have what it takes to be on the basketball team he wanted to be on. We all know that Michael Jordan is called the greatest basketball player of all time. However, before getting there, he first had to look at what was necessary for achieving his goals. In other words, in order to make the team and be good, he would be required to look at why the coach said that he did not have what it took. If the reasoning was that he was too short and skinny, he knew that he had to gain more weight and use his lack of height as an advantage by becoming stronger than others, being able to jump higher, and by becoming faster. He took what he did have and made it better, then worked to make up for what he lacked at the time. He had to break down his overall goals into small attainable pieces and make adjustments as he went to achieve his goal, thereby eliminating the barriers or breaking down the walls that could have created self-doubt. Above all, he did not allow the limitations that others placed on him to become his limitations.

Then there is the incredible and inspiring story of Maya Angelou—Writer, poet, performer, and director. In the mid-1930s her mother's boyfriend raped the seven-year-old Angelou. Traumatized by the whole experience, Angelou stopped speaking altogether, and she and her brother moved back to Arkansas. Through her study of writing, literature, and music, Angelou gained the will to speak again, and by the age of 12, she became known for her precocious intelligence. While attending high school, she won a scholarship in dance and drama to the California Labor School. Just after she graduated from high school in 1945, her son, Clyde "Guy" Johnson, was born. She held a succession of jobs in San Francisco and San Diego—where she worked as a nightclub waitress and as a madam for two prostitutes—and was turned down for enlistment in the United States Army. Encouraged by such prominent writers as James Baldwin and Jules Feiffer to write the story of her own life in the same lilting, powerful style in which she performed, Angelou published her first book, *I Know Why the Caged Bird Sings,* in 1970. The story of the first 17 years of her life, up until the birth of her son, the memoir met with astonishing critical acclaim and popular success. Since then, Angelou has become one of the most celebrated writers in America and a distinctive voice of African-American culture in particular. Angelou also gained worldwide renown as a poet. She was nominated for a Pulitzer Prize in 1971 for her first volume of verse, entitled *Just Give Me a Cool Drink of Water 'fore I Diiie.* Her poetry became phenomenally popular, especially such favorites as "Phenomenal Woman," and "Still I Rise." In January 1993, Angelou became the first poet since Robert Frost, in 1961, to take part in a presidential inauguration ceremony when she wrote and read "On the Pulse of Morning," at President Bill Clinton's inauguration. Her recording of the poem won Angelou a Grammy Award for Best Nonmusical Album. Angelou also read her poem, "A Brave and Startling Truth," for the 50th anniversary of the United Nations in 1995.

With some 50 honorary degrees at different institutions, Angelou reportedly commands $15,000 for speaking engagements. In 1981, she accepted a special lifetime appointment as a professor of American Studies at Wake Forest University in Winston-Salem, North Carolina. Angelou is fluent in French, Spanish, Italian, Arabic, and the West African language of Fanti.

Maya Angelou could have given up because of so many obstacles in her past. She was raped at an early age and stop speaking for sometime, she had a child at an early age, she was a nightclub waitress, a madam for two prostitutes—and was turned down for enlistment in the United States Army. How could this person, who had gone through so much negative stuff, ever believe that she would ever be anything thing in life and be accepted by anyone? Maya Angelou could have let others define who she was and how far in life she could go based on her past. Instead she used her past to get to where she wanted to be and to live out her purpose. She focused on what she could do rather than what she could not do, thereby breaking down the walls of self-doubt. Her story is a prime example of how we can still move on to achieve our goals, no matter where we are in life and what situations we find ourselves in, by keeping positive and focused on our abilities and not so much our circumstances.

Purpose and vision are the main resources you will need to break down the walls of self-doubt. We must approach these walls with the confidence of purpose and the insight of vision, which will serve as our jackhammer, ready to break down any wall. We must be willing to face these walls during frustration, tears, and pain, keeping in mind what we want and where we are going in life.

In the expanse of our lives, self-doubt is formed, because we have built thoughts and assumptions about who we are and where we are going, what we can and cannot do. Our encounters, experiences, mistakes, and interactions have built these thoughts and assumptions. We have built certain conclusions about ourselves based on these things, and those very conclusions and assumptions can be the obstacles and stumbling blocks that are preventing us from obtaining our dreams. These things may seem like facts in our minds, but that does not mean they are right. Your idea of yourself and who you are can offer great resistance when trying to achieve something that your mind tells you is too great for you to achieve. The assumptions that you have built up about yourself may be wrong, and you need to closely explore who you are before you dare go after that dream of who you want to become.

Plenty of walls of self-doubt and assumptions can be broken down simply by looking deeper into ourselves and discovering what we think and why we think that way regarding what we can and cannot do. Then we begin to let go of the negative "if only," "self-doubt," "self-comparisons," "and "self-judgments." We begin to accept the person in the mirror for who he or she is.

It takes courage to examine yourself closely, because once you do this, you also need the courage to start making changes in how you think about yourself. It takes great courage and determination to start breaking down the walls of self-doubt that, because of experiences, past mistakes, self-judgments, and comparisons to others, have limited our accomplishments.

In the end, all your experience and mistakes come together to make you who you are: a unique individual with a unique talent to bring to the table of this world. Consider all your past experiences and mistakes—the negative ones that presented you the opportunity to grow and the positive ones that gave you something to build on. Mix in all your acquired skills and lifelong knowledge and you will find that you already have what it takes to take that first step in achieving and going beyond your dreams. You are not whole without considering and accepting all of what you are. Once you have examined yourself from that standpoint, you can break down any wall of self-doubt. First, you remain focused on what you want. Second, you come face to face with that barrier or wall, looking deep into yourself and seeing what you already have that will help you overcome what you do not have. Learn from the past rather than becoming it. In our lives, we will make mistakes, we will fall and falter, but the greatest successes are born from those mistakes and problems, or our valley experiences.

Make a list of the things in your life that have caused self-doubt. Examine that list carefully and see how many of those were established by outside influences and how many are a result of self-imposed limitations, created by comparing yourself to others, past mistakes and negative circumstances. Take a look at what you want to achieve and make a list of your attributes that will help you achieve this goal. Then look at what you need to do to overcome the remaining barriers. Worry less about all the failures, but think about all the opportunities gained because of the failures. You have just started to break down your walls of self-doubt. Once we have learned to break down the walls of self-doubt and work on what and how we think of ourselves, we must then start building up walls of positive thinking that will help shape our attitude and self-confidence. In other words, we must start focusing on what we think about

CHAPTER SEVEN

BUILDING UP
POSITIVE WALLS
Attitude &
Self-Confidence

"WHAT WE THINK ABOUT"

When Joseph came to them the next morning, he saw that they were dejected, so he asked Pharaoh's officials who were in custody with him in his master's house, why are your faces so sad today? Tell me your dreams. . . .
                                                        —Genesis 40: 6-8

JOHN MILTON (1608-1674), one of the greatest poets of the English language, was best known for his epic poem "Paradise Lost." It tells a biblical story of Adam and Eve's fall and expulsion from Eden. He writes:

> *The mind is its own place, and in itself*
> *Can make a Heav'n of Hell,*
> *a Hell of Heav'n.*

That's powerful stuff: The mind is its own place and can make a Heaven out of Hell and a Hell out of Heaven. In other words, what we choose to put in our minds and dwell on will have a direct effect on our actual lives or our reality. What we choose to think about and dwell on actually determines our attitude and our attitude determines our destination. We have heard the advertisement, as it relates to drugs and education, that a mind is a terrible thing to waste. The mind is not only a terrible thing to waste, the mind is a powerful thing to use. The old saying remains true: What the mind perceives, we can achieve. If used incorrectly, it can cause the sudden death of our hopes, goals, and dreams. The reason many of us never reach our goals and never find fulfillment is because we have been thinking about the wrong things and surrounding ourselves with the wrong people. If we are to achieve any of what we spoke about in the previous chapters, it is up to us to be careful what we think about and to work on the way we think. Many of us do not effectively control our thoughts, and the things we allow our minds to dwell on will actually defeat us.

We wake each day with the responsibility of filling each moment that we are living. What we fill those moments with is up to us. Just by the way we think, we have the chance to decide what kind of day we will have. It does not matter too much what is going on around us as long as we have already decided that we are going to have a positive day. When we decide that we are only going to think about the positive instead of seeing a rainy day, we will see the beautiful flowers that resulted from the rain. Instead of being down because we are ill, we will be thankful that we are alive. A positive attitude will help us see loneliness as a reason to meet people. It will help you rejoice that you have a job, instead of grumbling because of the early hour alarm clock that wakes you to go to work. A positive attitude will help you appreciate the roof over your head, instead of the hard work required to keep everything under the roof clean.

We wake in the morning with a full twenty-four-hour day. Those twenty-four hours are ours to shape and mold as we see fit. No one else or nothing else should be able to take your place in shaping and molding your day; after all, at the end of the day, all that matters is how you shaped your day. We may not get to decide what will happen to us, but we can decide how we will respond. We can't decide what others will do, but we can determine our reaction. Our thinking can affect an entire day.

By keeping a positive attitude, Joseph was given positions of great responsibility, including being declared second in charge of Egypt. Nothing besides faith and a positive attitude could have allowed this man to hold onto his dreams while he was being sold as a slave and imprisoned. His response, action and reaction during turbulent times demonstrates that it matters what we think about. Our thoughts build our attitudes and with a positive attitude, we will conclude that we can make it through any situation.

God remained with Joseph because Joseph held on to his purpose in life, which was given to him through his dreams. What purpose would there be for God to hang around if Joseph had given up all hope in God, himself, and his dreams? Joseph helped the other men interpret their dreams, showing his faith in God and confidence in himself. He chose to believe that he still could, no matter what his situation, become a person of great power, prestige, and honor. That attitude shone through to all that placed him in positions of responsibility. What he thought is what he became.

Proverbs 23:7, in suggesting that we should be careful not to keep company with a certain kind of person, also suggest that as people think in their heart, so are they. What we put in our minds, we can then become, but that has good and bad ramifications. The good is that if we fill our minds with the positive, we can become positive; the other side is that if we fill our minds with the negative and dwell on it, we can become negative. It suggests that whatever you put in your mind becomes part of your heart and part of you if it remains there long enough. It is no longer just a passing thought, it is now residing within you. Our success or failure relies on how we think and what we think about. The mind helps move you closer to your dreams or the mind can make your dreams unreachable. The mind can see the silver lining or the mind can give up all hope.

There was a story I once heard told by Reverend Frederick Haynes that clarifies my point about our thinking. I have not validated this story but it was supposedly featured in the news. Nevertheless, it is a very valuable story and it relates directly to our discussion. In Siberia, a waiter on a passenger train was sent by the chef to get some frozen meat from a refrigerator boxcar. As he entered the car to get the meat, the spring actuated door slammed shut behind him. The slam of the door reminded him with terror that the door locked from the outside and could not be opened from the inside.

Immediately, the waiter concluded that he was going to freeze to death. With the mindset that he was going to die, his teeth began to chatter and goosebumps began forming all over his body. In panic, he started beating loudly on the door until he remembered that the refrigerated boxcar was soundproof. He concluded that unless someone noticed shortly that he was missing, he would surely die.

After an hour passed, the waiter had given up; he'd already settled in his mind that there was no way he would be rescued before he froze to death. So, with that thought, he grabbed a marker he had found, and he began to write on the wall, leaving messages to his family and friends. When two hours had gone by and he had written several notes, it is said that he then decided to write one last note. That last note simply said, "Goodbye, cruel world" and before he could write the D at the end of world, he slumped over and died in the refrigerator boxcar.

Shortly after the train came to a stop, the chef realized that the waiter had not brought back the meat; he then sent someone to see if the waiter was all right. Upon unlocking and opening the refrigerator boxcar door, the person was met by two very different smells. The first was that of spoiled meat and the other was the smell of death. He discovered that the meat had spoiled because the thermostat on the refrigerator boxcar was broken—it was sixty-five degrees in the car.

The waiter had died thinking that it was less than twenty degrees below zero. He died tragically, not because he froze to death, but because he thought himself to death.

This story does a fine job of illustrating the power of the mind as well as the meaning of John Milton's statement that the mind can make a Heaven out of Hell and a Hell out of Heaven. The mind that shapes our attitudes also shapes the today in which we live. It can hold us down or it can give us flight. The mind can destroy us or it can give us life through purpose. Just like the waiter, we can think ourselves hopeless and out of the race of life or we can choose to fill our minds with purpose and hope. We must ask ourselves what is in our minds. What are we thinking about? Moreover, is what we are thinking about conducive to where we want to go?

In Philippians, the apostle Paul mention things worthy of thinking about:

> *Finally brothers whatever is true,*
> *whatever is noble,*
> *whatever is right,*
> *whatever is pure,*
> *whatever is lovely,*
> *whatever is admirable –*
> *If anything is excellent*
> *or praiseworthy-*
> *think on such things.*
>
> —Philippians 4:8

Many of us will have major breakthroughs in life just by changing our thinking. We look to books and doctors to help us change the way we think, but it's up to us to change our own thinking from dwelling on the negative to focusing on the positive. Paul says in the above verse that we should learn to think and dwell or meditate on those things that are true, honest, just, pure, lovely, of good report or positive news, of virtue and praise. We need to take note of those we surround our selves with and what we listen to and accept as right or wrong, good or bad. What we put in our minds determines what comes out in our words and actions. Paul tells us to program our minds and only medi-tate on or think thoughts that are uplifting, motivating, inspiring, and noteworthy. We should examine what we are putting into our minds through television, books, movies, and magazines. Let us be determined to replace harmful input with those things that will further our cause of reaching our goals and seeing our dreams through to reality.

Let us also set good examples for our children in the type of entertainment we seek. Their minds are still forming and impressionable. What we put into their heads now will most assuredly affect their future actions. Movies and video games do not have to be violent or immoral to be entertaining. Is it just coincidence that the increase in these types of leisure activities has led to an increase in violent acts by children? Something to consider.

Over the course of time, we all become who we are because of the choices we have made in life. I must reiterate that we are completely responsible for where we are today. We're here because of the decisions we made, and we made those decisions based upon our own beliefs, what we think, and how we think. In turn, our choices are based upon how we think and what we think about; therefore, our thinking forms our mentality, our attitude. Our attitude then determines how far we go in life.

This attitude, then, is the way we think about our lives and ourselves, our experiences, environment, opportunities, and problems. It is our approach to and outlook on life. It is the main reason we act or react the way we do to life's issues. It affects the way we feel about ourselves and those around us as well as what we choose to accept or not to accept, the opinions we form, and our philosophy on life. I call my philosophy on life "Drakology." This is my point of view and opinions formed from my experiences, studies, and what I think. It is what I choose to accept as truth; it is my own thinking that make up who I am and what I am to become.

Our attitude begins as thoughts. Then, as time goes on, those thoughts form and build our attitude or, as I call them, walls of habit. There are good and positive walls of habit and there are negative walls of habit. Initially, we are unconscious to their existence, but once we are aware that they are there, we then have the choice to either be a servant to them or make them a servant to our success. Because our attitude is so important and reflects our actual thinking, it is extremely important to control what we think about. Our attitude establishes possibilities as well as limitations or impossibilities. Our attitude can be positive and a great ally in our journey to success or it can be a great ally to our failure. Thus, a positive attitude is necessary in order to believe that no matter what life throws our way, we can handle it. While the positive attitude sees the silver lining in the middle of the storm, the negative attitude will see only how bad the storm is. Positive attitudes *make* life happen and negative attitudes let life happens.

While we cannot be responsible for what others do or think, nor how they act or react in any given situation, we can control what we choose to think about and how we act or react to situations in life. We must have and learn to develop a positive mind. We need to learn to move away from negative people and negative things and stop listening to negative music and looking at negative TV programs. We must be positive thinkers and surround ourselves with positive things and learn to turn negative things into positive things. You see, in our lives we are going to make some bad choices; we are going to make some awful mistakes. However, it is up to us to turn those mistakes into the steps that will get us where we are going. We must be the ones to get up, shake it off, and move forward. If we successfully and consistently work on positive thinking, then our positive attitudes will never let anyone hold us down, regardless of our past mistakes, problems, or bad decisions. A positive attitude will allow us to decide in our mind that we made a bad decision or that something was a mistake, then accept the responsibility for that mistake and move forward.

People may try to discourage you or hold you back because of your past or because of bad choices you have made. Then there are those that will be there to cheer us on. Understand that while it is good to have others beside us, cheering us on, it is ultimately up to us. We establish within our own minds how far we can go. We must set our own limits instead of letting situations or other people set them for us. It is our life, our dream, and our choice. If we are not where we want to be, we then need to reevaluate where our minds are. With the positive attitude that comes only from persistence, constancy, and hardwork, nothing or no one should be able to strip us of our belief in ourselves.

I cannot stress enough, as we discussed in a previous chapter, the importance of putting the past behind us as memories and lessons learned rather than making them today's thoughts. Examine the full array of possibilities for today and tomorrow. As the seasons change, we see the flowers disappear and leaves on the trees change color and drift to the ground in the fall and the winter, but in the spring and summer, we see a regeneration of sorts, where new flowers arise and new leaves grow. So must we: We must concentrate on rebuilding ourselves fully—mentally, spiritually, and physically. We must rebuild old negative thinking with fresh positive thinking and use past troubles and mistakes as possibilities for today and tomorrow, using them to help build greater awareness and steadfast determination. This creates in us a greater focus for our lives and a more positive attitude about where we are and where we are going.

If we are to work on and build up our wall of positive attitude and self-confidence, we must affirm and reaffirm what it is that we want each day. We must break down the affirmations that are destructive and negative to us and build on the positive ones that are conducive to growth and success. The negative affirmations are there to stagnate and destroy while the positive affirmation stands to motivate, inspire, and build us up. Again, if what is in our minds is not productive, then it can only be destructive and we need to replace it with the positive. It is the positive thoughts and the positive things around us that shape how we view life and ourselves in any given situation. Once inspired and built up strong, our attitudes will be one of our greatest resources in overcoming the negative thoughts of why we can't do something.

Take time now to write down something positive, a positive affirmation that will serve as a reminder of where you are going and a motivation and inspiration that says you can achieve whatever your mind perceives. This should be something that dispels the negative and builds upon the positive. Let me share my daily affirmation with you:

> *I have what it takes on the inside of me to be all that I can*
> *   and all that I am:*
> *to mount on wings of eagles to overcome any obstacle.*
> *Those that I can't go over, I will go around and those*
> *   I can't go around,*
> *I will gladly go through, knowing that it can only make me stronger.*
> *I will not give in, because I do have a purpose in life,*
> *and that purpose must be lived through me and by me.*

The reaffirming thought you say each day can prove to be most powerful when the very things you break down, self-doubt, try to

reemerge and during the times when that self-doubt and outside negative influences threaten to stop us in our tracks. We must believe what
we are saying, where we are trying to go, and then stand on the faith
of the purpose for our lives.

Your self-confidence will come from understanding yourself and
what it is that you have to contribute. In other words, what is so special
about you. You should take the time to define what makes you special
and unique, what it is that you like to do, and what you have that others may not. Perhaps you have the patience to work with kids or the
gift to speak in front of large audiences, the patience to teach or the
insight to counsel. From this, you will gain the self-confidence to realistically determine what it is you want and should be doing in life.

We must use our full imagination and move beyond just thinking
to thinking outside of the typical box if we are to see ourselves or imagine ourselves already achieving our dreams. It is not so much the
dream itself that motivates and excites us, but the thought of us living
and achieving our dreams and believing that we actually have a place
in life, a purpose. It is seeing through our mind's eyes what our life
could be and will be like when our dreams are fulfilled. It's a great feeling to wake up each day with the determination to make a difference.

The Christians press on, looking forward to and imagining the day
that they are taken to Heaven where there will be no more tears, fears, or
dying. The thought of being in Heaven with God propels them and provides greater determination in pressing toward that mark. It does so in a
way that they model their lives after their calling and they surround themselves with that thought of their greater reward in Heaven. In this way,
their calling translates into a way of life. The pursuit of our purpose must
become a way of life for us and not just a daydream or a distant thought.

Now, with all this said, it is important to understand that the positive attitude does not provide carte blanche to easy street beyond life's
troubles or a ticket to bypass the problems of life. It does, however, go
a long way in helping us deal with life's issues and makes us better able
to cope with obstacles that stand in our way. A positive attitude affirms
to you and declares to the world that we cannot be conquered by circumstances. It reaffirms in us that it is not so much what is going on
around us, but what is going on in our minds that is important.

As we end this discussion, the final analysis is that we must take
charge of our thoughts, filling our lives and our minds with those

things that are conducive to a positive attitude. Instead of complaining, making excuses, and resisting and fighting changes in our lives, we will be able to accept both the good and bad in our lives. We will be able to see those obstacles and problems as challenges and opportunities. This must be the only way to think if we are driven by our dreams that hold the key to the purpose of our lives.

I provide diversity training to different organizations, that's the acceptance and appreciation of others and their differences. The training teaches that we need to respect what others bring to the table and, with regard to our topic, it starts with what we choose to believe and think. That appreciation for others, including their race and cultures, can be damaged based on what we have allowed ourselves to think about others around us and by what we choose to keep in our minds, such as stereotypes. To illustrate this point and conclude this chapter, I'd like to share a poem I use in my training:

THE COLD WITHIN

Six humans trapped by happenstance
In dark and bitter cold
Each one possessed a stick of wood,
Or so the story's told.

Their dying fire in need of logs,
The first women held hers back.
For on the faces around the fire,
She noticed one was black.

The next man looking 'cross the way,
Saw one not of his church,
And couldn't bring himself to give
The fire his stick of birch.

The third one sat in tattered clothes,
He gave his coat a hitch.
Why should his log be put to use,
To warm the idle rich?

The rich man just sat back and thought
Of the wealth he had in store.
And how to keep what he had earned
From the lazy, shiftless poor.

The black man's face bespoke revenge
As the fire passed from sight,
For all he saw in his stick of wood
Was a chance to spite the white.

The last man of this forlorn group
Did naught except for gain.
Giving only to those who gave
Was how he played the game.

The logs held tight in death's still hands
Was proof of human sin.
They didn't die from the cold without,
They died from — THE COLD WITHIN.

—Author Unknown

Another unknown poet put it like this:

If you think you are beaten, you are.
If you think you dare not, you don't.
If you like to win and think you can't, you won't.
It is almost a cinch you won't.
If you think you are outclassed, you are.
You got to think high to rise;
You got to be sure of yourself before you could ever win a prize.
Life battles do not always go to the faster or stronger man,
But sooner or later, the man who wins is the one who thinks he can.

Both poems effectively illustrate that our success and failure—outlook and outcome, depends greatly on our attitude and what we chose to think about. The one who wins and succeeds in life is not always the faster or stronger, but the one who believes that they can.

CHAPTER EIGHT

JUST DO IT

Commitment &
Self -Control

So Pharaoh said to Joseph, "I hereby put you in charge of the whole land of Egypt."

                                                                    —Genesis 41:41

"JUST DO IT" is the Nike sneaker commercial theme that dares us to stop just thinking about doing something, but take the initiative and actually do what we have been dreaming about. All that you see around you—Microsoft Systems, Wal-mart stores, Marriott hotels, and the small shops on the corners—were dreams in the minds and hearts of the people that started them. In order for those dreams to become reality, those people had to step beyond just the dream in their heads and move it to their hearts so that they could put it into action. In other words, once they had the dream, they had to dare to go beyond that dream and just do it. To just do it with regard to our life's purpose requires that we commit ourselves to the task and then maintain the self-control to consistently work at that goal.

So now you have all these wonderful thoughts in your head and the excitement of making those thoughts a reality is overwhelming. These overwhelming thoughts are often the culprits that talk us out of making those thoughts anything more. Now is the time to just do it. Dig deep down on the inside of you, look for the motivation, and pull that inspiration out to commit to making your dreams real. We all have what it takes to go beyond the thought of living out our dreams. Those that are successful, I mean those that are truly happy living their lives doing what they do, have learned to pull on the inner motivation to propel them beyond mere thought and talk of their dreams and have found through their purpose the inspiration to stay committed.

It is said that the hardest part about doing anything is the act of actually getting started. I find this especially true in writing this book, my first. I believe, as you will see, that the next books I write will flow much smoother, but the hardest part was just getting started. It was particularly difficult because I spent too much time looking at the enormity of the job ahead, so much so that it stagnated me. From start to finish, there were so many things to do in writing and getting this book published that it not only stagnated me, it scared me into inaction. It was hard working the long hours at night and spending the early mornings writing and gathering information while still having to work, be a father and a husband, and fulfill my spiritual obligations. I should have completed this book long ago, but the thought of all the work involved and the uncertainty of how others would accept the content of this book held me back while time still marched on.

The funny thing about time is that it does not wait for you to just do it, it will move with or without you; it could be in your favor or against you, but ultimately, even though we can't stop or pause time, we can use it to our benefit. To use time to our benefit is to use time wisely by taking advantage of every opportunity to do something that will get us closer to our goals. However, in order to convince ourselves to use that time to do something that we want to do, to have a life beyond the normal things that we do to make a living, is no small task.

By writing this book, I would be accomplishing one of my goals toward realizing my dreams and purpose in life—to motivate and inspire people, through both spoken and written words, to be the very best that they can be. In addition to living out my purpose and working to achieve my dreams through writing this book, I still had to continue working and making a living in the meantime. That meant sacrificing the little extra time that I had each day, somehow creating extra time to achieve these goals. Well, as you may already know, it takes some self-convincing to sacrifice our already scarce time by doing something that is not yet the primary means for bringing home the bacon. I needed something that would convince me not only that I could do it, but also that it was worth the sacrifice. In accomplishing these goals and striving to realize my dreams, there had to be a factor that would persuade me that not only could I be committed to my goals, but that I would have the self-control to see them to completion. This factor must be the thing that will move me from inaction to action, from doubt to motion. I stated earlier in my introduction that it is my hope that this book will serve to motivate you to action and be the catalyst that will spark your inspiration for living out your true potential.

We need that motivation and inspiration to go beyond our dreams. What does that mean? Where do I get it? And how do I get it? Different things in life trigger that unique something—already on the inside of us—that will motivate us. For me, it is seeing or reading about Dr. Martin Luther King Jr. and what he had to endure to achieve greatness and live out his purpose. It is reading the story of Joseph in the Bible and knowing that God has a purpose for all our lives. It is seeing the hope in the eyes of an audience when I speak about living out the true meaning of our lives. It is also seeing tragedy in life and knowing that I have what it takes to make a difference and can do a better job than some for the good of all. It is the motivation that will help you turn the ideas into good intentions and will help you take the first steps in achieving your dreams, but it will be the inspiration that will keep you motivated and focused and that will turn the intentions into committed actions.

To be motivated is to have a motive, need, or desire that causes a person to act and to be inspired—the action or power of moving the intellect or emotions and to influence, move, or guide by divine or supernatural inspiration. Just seeing people spending their lives making a living, but never having a life, can motivate me to do something about it, like write this book. However, unless I believe that it is my purpose to help people live out their dreams, the motivation to do so may only be temporary. Without purpose, or what I call a higher calling, any of us can get motivated for a moment by anything. It is that inspiration that will keep us focused while going through valley experiences during the meanwhile period and it is inspiration that will help us say we can when other say that we cannot. When we are inspired, we will find it easier to take responsibility for our own actions, good, bad, or indifferent, so that we can move forward to accept the lessons learned from those situations. The inspiration will provide the endurance and persistence to knock down the walls of self-doubt caused by past experiences, people, and situations, and that same inspiration will help us control what we think and dwell on to build positive walls of attitude and self-confidence. When we are motivated, we will take the first steps down the road of achieving our dreams; with inspiration, those first steps will turn into more determined steps that will help us continue down that road.

We can see that there is a difference between good intentions created by motivation and commitment created by our inspiration. Our good intentions without commitment can remain a thought or just a first step, but, when mixed with commitment, good intentions turn thoughts into actions and long-term positive results. Commitment is your sincere promise to and belief in yourself and a great willingness to do whatever it takes to obtain what you want. So many people have great dreams and intentions without commitment, and, likewise, our dreams will remain only a thought or incomplete action if we are not willing to do whatever it takes to make that sincere promise to our-selves to commit to the achievement of those dreams.

If what you want to achieve in life is worthwhile for you to do what-ever it takes, is something you want badly enough, and you will pay whatever price it costs to achieve it, then that is the formula for com-mitment. Your dreams will be achieved based on the degree of your commitment and your dedication to making time, instead of waiting for time to appear, so that you can accomplish your goals. We have time for those things that we like, but we must also make the time for the things we sincerely want.

I feel it is important to once again say a few words about our friend, Joseph. All the things that we have read about him and have said about him come to this end. In order for him to go through what he did and for him to maintain a positive mind and confidence in his God-given dreams and talents, I believe that he had to believe in his purpose in life. He had to be inspired in order to hold on to his dreams throughout his ordeal. Motivation may have moved him to tell his brothers all about his dreams, but inspiration helped him to hold on to those dreams while he was thrown in a pit, sold into slavery, false-ly accused of rape and thrown into jail, and forgotten by those he helped. That inspiration came from his belief in a higher purpose for his life and that inspiration continually fed his motivation. Both are very important and all-inclusive; it may be impossible to reach your goals or live out your purpose by using only one or the other. In other words, our motivation is fed by our inspiration, which is in turn fed by our belief in our God-given purpose.

The lack of this commitment produces a life full of repetitiveness with goals of only getting by. People whose lives are not filled with commitment rise in the morning only to complain about their plight and spend their day majoring in the minors, reducing themselves far below their own capabilities.

Commitment is like a vaccine against difficulties, obstacles, and perceptions, because it plants in you the will to press on no matter what comes your way. It helps you to never give up or become frus-trated when you fall or falter. We can have all the great dreams and good intentions in the world, and even have the resources to help make them come true, but without commitment, the achievements of the dreams and the actions of good intentions may never be seen.

One other example of motivation, inspiration, and commitment is the story of Peter walking on water. The disciples of Jesus were out on a boat in the Sea of Galilee when they encountered a storm. They saw Jesus walking on the water toward them. When Peter saw him, he called out, "If it is you, then let me come out to you." Jesus told him to come to him. Peter stepped off the boat and began walking on the water toward Jesus. He began to sink because he focused more on the strong winds around him and lost focus of where he was going. This story is one that deals with faith; however, it also deals with our motivations and inspirations. Seeing Jesus walk on water motivated Peter and his motivation moved him to take the first steps on water toward Jesus. But as I stated earlier, motivation by itself may only be temporary and not enough to go against all that we face. Our good intentions must be turned into committed actions by something stronger than just motivation. Peter needed the inspiration that came from Christ, which let him know that all things are possible, to avoid being sidetracked by what was going on around him.

If you get a chance to read further about Peter, you will see that in the beginning, he was motivated to follow and learn from his relationship with Jesus. With motivation only, he not only began to sink when he was walking on water, but he denied Jesus three times. Later in his life, when he was inspired by the life of Jesus and believed that he had a purpose in the ministry of Jesus, he was a changed man. Circumstance and surroundings no longer distracted him from his cause. He was brought before the court for standing up for what he believed in and he spoke boldly, without succumbing. He was thrown in jail for those same beliefs.

People who combine motivation with inspiration find their motivation continually fed and distractions turn into steps to get to where they are going. We must allow the gift that is inside of us, given by the Creator, to inspire and feed the motivation that will help us to take the first steps of living a committed and fulfilled life.

CHAPTER NINE

THE DREAM
REALIZED
Direction

And now, do not be distressed and do not be angry with yourselves for selling
me here, because it was to save lives that God sent me ahead of you . . . So then
it was not you who sent me here but God. He made me father to Pharaoh, Lord
of his entire household and ruler of all Egypt.
—Genesis 45:5,8

WE CAN DO so many things once we realize that our lives do have purpose and that there is more to life than just making a living. This book
only scratches the surface, but, as stated earlier in the introduction, I
hope that it will start a self-dialogue as to what you are to do once you
have discovered your purpose. In doing so, I would like to offer a few
suggestions. Up to this point, we have mainly spoken about all the
internal things that we need to do to first understand that we have a
purpose, to look for that purpose deep within ourselves, and to use
our actions to hold on to and live out that purpose. We discussed the
things in life we most want to do; deciding to work on the confidence
to start doing them today; understanding the value of our hard times
in helping us endure and be persistent through our valley experiences; accepting responsibility for where we are; breaking down walls
of self-doubt so that we can begin to build the walls of positive thinking; and using self-confidence and higher commitment levels to
achieve what we want through inspiration and motivation.

The following things will help you live a rich and fulfilled life after
you have become inspired and motivated to live out your purpose.
They will help strengthen you spiritually, mentally, and physically on
your life mission.

Lend a Helping Hand.
It is my belief that we cannot truly be the very best that we can without
first helping others be the best they can be. Our purpose in life, the fulfillment of our dreams, should not be only to lift and serve ourselves, but
to help and lift others. We will not find any great people in history whose
sole purpose was to serve themselves or to be self-serving. They were
great because their purpose in life, their gift, was to help or serve others.
Each of us has a special gift and that gift was given so that we might
enrich not only our own lives, but share it with the rest of the world.

Can you imagine how many people have lived and died without
ever sharing their true gifts or talents with the world? How rich we

would all be if each of us would share our special talents. Look how much better off Michael Jordan's dream has made the game of basketball. Look how much better off the church is to have had Martin Luther King Jr. live out his purpose and give us all hopes and dreams of a better tomorrow. Pilgrims in search of religious freedom, not self-gain, have helped us as a country. The singers, politicians, preachers, teachers, and counselors all have special talents that we would miss out on if they were not shared. One of the greatest commandments says it best: Love your neighbor as you love yourself.

I received a story over the Internet where the volunteer of a hospital was telling a story of a little girl she had gotten to know. She said that this little girl was suffering from a rare and serious disease whereby her only chance of recovery would be a blood transfusion from her five-year-old brother. Her brother had survived the same disease and had developed the antibodies needed to combat the illness. The little boy, after having the situation explained to him by the doctor, was asked if he would be willing to give his blood to his sister. With a slight hesitation and a deep breath, the little boy agreed to do it in order to save his sister. He lay in bed next to his sister and smiled as the transfusion started to work and he saw the color returning to his sister's face. Then, all of a sudden, his face grew pale and his smile faded. He looked up at the doctor and asked with a trembling voice, "Will I start to die right away?" The young boy had misunderstood the doctor; he thought he was going to have to give his sister all his blood.

If we are to grow and live to be the very best that we can be, then we must also be willing to help others grow and live to be their very best. Reaching out to others boosts our own confidence and abilities and can make a world of difference in someone's life.

Set Good Examples.
Always remember that no matter what you do, there is someone watching. Your life can be the catalyst that will help motivate and inspire others to do something great with their lives. Children are a prime example. With our actions, we should show them how to be confident, giving, goal-seeking adults. They can learn from either our direction or our misdirection. The choice is ours, but it affects more than just us.

Take One Day at a Time.
We can only live one day at a time, so there is no use worrying about

what will happen the day after tomorrow. Sure, we have to schedule events on our calendar for days and months ahead, but once they are scheduled, spend your time working on the things that count today and that will lead you into tomorrow. When we start trying to do everything at once, we can easily become frustrated and very little ends up getting done.

A college student can cram for a test until he knows the material inside and out. Afterward, he can worry that he doesn't know enough, causing himself undue stress over the impending exam, or he can start studying for the next one.

Setting Goals - Put it in Writing.
Get Started.
Goal setting is extremely important when reaching for your dreams, but it is equally important to understand that your main satisfaction will result from working to achieve your goals. Checking off the items and smaller goals that will ultimately get you to where you want to be is very rewarding and motivating.

After you have decided where you want to go or what you want to achieve, break it down into small goals. Be realistic as to what you can do in the time frame you allot for each goal. The goals should challenge you, but not overtake you.

One you have written them down, take a moment to prioritize your goals into short-term, medium-term, and long-term goals. Then, prioritize in each category the ones that make the most sense to complete first and the ones that interest you most. If you come across ones that seem too large, impossible, or don't interest you, get rid of them if they are unnecessary. If they are essential to your purpose, break them down into smaller obtainable goals. One problem many of us face is that we have too many goals and become overwhelmed. Look at your list carefully and make sure that those goals that we give equal value to cannot be changed or eliminated, so that we will not be shifting attention between one goal and another. Start with three to five goals that are most meaningful and then focus on them. Again, if some goals are unimportant, you may have to let them go.

Now you'll need to do something that takes a little more concentration, time, and effort. Take time to write down your plans for achieving each one of your goals. This will serve as your blueprint and will increase your commitment to that goal. It serves as your promise or contract to yourself. Once you get used to seeing your goals and the blueprint to achieving them, you will also become used to seeing yourself achieving them. Try starting with the first three and writing out how you will achieve them. Then, write out in detail how you will achieve the next few goals. You can and are advised to look at them on a regular basis, making changes as you go along. It is like a business plan for your life where you have to makes changes as situations or events affect how you will reach your goals.

Realize that these goals are set within the timeframes you felt you were able to realistically complete in time. Note in your mind that the timeframes are only estimates and not an exact science and can change due to situations beyond your control that may happen to move you off that timeline. If we are to obtain our goals, they require careful planning and commitment, but it is foolish to believe that there will not be obstacles and unexplained challenges along the way. We must have the flexibility to alter our plans and shift our goals in order to stay on course and not become another statistic of failure. We must pay close attention to our goals and plans so as not to be so constrained in our planning that an obstacle or delay will move that goal out of reach and throw us into a state of despair. Be flexible with your goals and do not give up or throw in the towel if you do not complete some of them in the time frame you planned. Let your written goals be a guide, not a master over you.

This paper containing your goals and dreams has set you apart from those that have dreams and do nothing about them. It now places you in the minority group of people who are willing to dream and then commit themselves to the achievement of those dreams no matter what it takes. Every day or as often as possible, make sure you review and affirm what you have written. Seeing the same words repeatedly will enforce them and make them a part of your life.

In writing this book, I was hesitant at first to let anyone read my manuscript, because I was uncertain whether I would be able to take the criticism others might have of my work. After all, I had worked very hard to complete my book. Who were they to judge or critique my work? That kind of attitude could have doomed my book from the start; the same people who would have provided advice would be the same kind of people to buy and read my book. Their advice could be what I needed to write a book that was worth your time. Never become so narrow-minded with your goals that you are not willing to hear other ideas. Keep a close eye on your destination, but be open to more than one way of getting there.

Do Your Homework—
Never Stop Learning.
Build Yourself Up.
Research the tools and resources you need to achieve each goal. One thing I do to help me achieve my goals is to build on my communication skills and my vocabulary. I am committed to learning at least twelve new words each week and then using them in my everyday interactions. Once you have decided what it is that you want to do and have written down your goals, take time to do your homework. Research what it takes to get to where you want to go. Do not become one of many statistics that fail to reach their goals because of bad planning and lack of knowledge. Life is a learning process, which can be frustrating, but also very exciting. If you continue to learn, you'll remain open-minded and motivated enough to follow your dreams.

Learn and Use
Time Management Skills.
Time can be your best friend or your worst enemy in reaching your goals. If you manage your time wisely, it will work in your favor. Schedule time to work on your most important goals during the times you have the most energy. Categorize the demands on your time and make sure that the things taking up your important time are necessary and that your "must do" things are your focus. We can get confused and believe that the things we like to do and the things we should do are the things we must do. The things we like to do are just that: They are things we would like to do and should make time for, but not during our important time. The things that we should do are things that we can do, providing that we have the time to do them, but not during our important time. The things we must do are the things that are responsibility related and are important to achieving our goals. These are the things we make time for during our important times of the day, when we have the most energy. Manage your time around your "to do" categories and the priorities you assign them.

Stay Focused.

As much as possible, avoid getting diverted—don't avoid doing the big things or important things to do the small things. I call this majoring in the minors. We will stop focusing on what must be done or the things that matter to take care of things that can wait, such as cleaning out our files, reading or writing e-mail, or making phone calls. While these things should be done, the time you set aside for the major goals is not the time to take care of them.

Keep away from the negative, including family, friends, movies, and music. Naysayers and negative images only detract us from our goals. If we hear often enough that we cannot do it, we may start to believe it. Anyone who minimizes the importance of your goals and dreams is not worth spending time with.

Understand that it is okay not to be perfect, that there is more than one right way to do things, and that you don't know everything. In other words, being a perfectionist can keep you from accomplishing your goals and make you miss the big picture. You can lose sight of your overall goal and start focusing on the smaller individual goals. There is nothing wrong with doing the very best you can and producing something that is less than perfect, but human.

Procrastination is another one of life's curves that can take our focus and direct our attention onto something else. It will lead us to doing nothing or to doing things that have nothing to do with our goals. Some typical procrastination tools include watching television, checking e-mail, talking on the phone, reading books that will distract us from our focus, and so on. We can very easily fall into a hard-to-break habit of procrastinating. We come home and instead of getting to work on our goals, we sit down in front of the television. Before we know it, we no longer have time for what is important. We must break this cycle by being determined to do something each day, no matter how small, to further our goals. When I was writing this book, I would sometimes sit in front of the computer screen and nothing would come to mind. So, instead of doing something to stimulate thought, I would turn on the television, check e-mail, and do other things that distracted me. It is very important to maintain self-discipline and to surround ourselves with things that help keep us focused.

Nourish the Full You—Body, Mind, and Spirit.

During the course of writing this book, there were moments when I just did not feel like writing or I needed something to stimulate or motivate me. I would take some much-needed quiet time for myself and read a good book or exercise. This is different than allowing needless distractions to deter your goals. These things helped me relax or release frustration, thereby stimulating thought.

Spend some regular quiet time by yourself, time that is controlled by you and that is yours alone. If possible, claim a part of the house that is yours alone for a certain period of time so that you can relax, pray, meditate, or do whatever else relaxes you and has no responsibility attached to it. You can use this time to stop and smell the roses, go on a picnic, go to the museum, get outdoors, and enjoy the beauty of God's creation. Finish a book that you have been reading or just have a leisurely non-stressing phone conversation with a friend. Again, please remember to not use this time for busy work or fill it with things that have responsibility attached to them.

Spend some time taking care of your body each day, even if it is just taking a walk. If you make the time to take care of it, your body will better take care of you when you are burning the midnight oil and getting up early in the morning to go again. If you are going to be demanding on your body, then be equally demanding of yourself when it comes time to take care of your body. Do exercises that will increase your stamina and endurance. Find a regular routine that is suited just for you.

Another aspect of taking care of your body is watching what you eat. Take time to plan and follow a healthy diet. Your diet can and will have a direct bearing on how you feel and will directly affect your energy level.

Take time to feed your spirit, the essence of who you are. Spend time with your Creator in prayer and study. This is one of the most important things you can do. Take time out each day to pray and meet with God. One thing that I do upon waking is to take a few moments to read from my Old Testament. I take a few moments at lunch to read my Psalms or Proverbs and take time in the evening for prayer and a study of my New Testament. It takes time and effort to set up a program that will fit you, but it is very rewarding. Remember that your attitude, which is shaped by what you think, is determined and fed by your spirituality. It is your spirituality or your proximity to goodness that will provide you with the inspiration to pursue your life's purpose.

Keep Good Company.
We all know the saying that we are only as good as the company we keep. It bears repeating that we should be selective of those we surround ourselves with; that company will either motivate or discouragement us. Not everyone, even some family and friends, will provide the positive energy necessary for success.

This chapter is intended to provide some of my thoughts and experiences for things that can help us in the pursuit of our dreams. The suggestions are limited in scope, but are only intended to get us thinking about the things that will aid us as individuals after we have discovered exactly what we want to do in life. It is my hope that I have successfully gotten you to think about an individualized plan that includes exercise, quiet time, and spiritual well-being, things that will help you once you have committed to taking the journey to fulfillment. However, it is now up to you to take all that we have discussed and use it to be all that you can and were created to be.

CHAPTER TEN

TOMORROW
Footprints or
If Only I...

YOU HAVE HEARD me say repeatedly that it is more important to be working toward our dreams than it is to actually achieve them. You have heard it said that our fulfillment is in the journey just as much as it is in the destination. My dad was completely happy doing what he did, not because he had obtained or achieved all that he wanted in life, but because he was living his dreams by working toward them. The Apostle Paul says:

> *Not that I have already obtained all this, or have been made perfect,*
> *but I press on to take hold of that which Christ Jesus took hold of me.*
> *Brothers I do not consider myself yet to have taken hold of it.*
> *But one thing I do: Forgetting what is behind and straining toward*
> *what is ahead, I press on toward the goal to win the prize*
> *for which God has called me heavenward in Christ Jesus.*
>
> —Philippians 3:12-14

Paul says that he knows where he should be and all that he is purposed to become, but that he is not there yet. Although he has yet to reach his goals, he continues to press on and take hold of what he was purposed for. To do this, he must forget what is behind him and strain toward what is ahead. In other words, yesterdays accomplishments, problems, obstacles, mistakes, and heartaches are just that, the past. He says that we must put those things where they belong, behind us, so that we can press toward what is left to do and what is ahead of us, the mark of the higher calling: our purpose in life. His words tell us that we may not reach our mark, but it is important to know that we can still fulfill our purpose in life by working toward our purpose. It is the joy of the journey, even more than the destination, that gives us fulfillment, focus, and purpose.

Earlier, I shared a snippet of the poem "A Psalm of Life," published in 1863 by the talented Henry Wadsworth Longfellow. Its insight bears repeating. It reveals the importance of taking advantage of the precious times in life before it is too late. He writes:

> *Tell me not, in mournful numbers,*
> *"Life is but an empty dream!"*
> *For the soul is dead that slumbers,*
> *And things are not what they seem.*

Life is real! Life is earnest!
And the grave is not its goal;
"Dust thou art, to dust returnest,"
Was not spoken of the soul.

Not enjoyment, and not sorrow,
Is our destined end or way;
But to act, that each to-morrow
Finds us farther than to-day.

Art is long, and Time is fleeting,
And our heart, though stout and brave,
Still, like muffled drums, are beating
Funeral marches to the grave.

In the world's broad field of battle,
In the bivouac of Life,
Be not like dumb, driven cattle!
Be a hero in the strife!

Trust no Future, howe'er pleasant!
Let the dead Past bury its dead!
Act, -act in the living Present!
Heart within, and God o'erhead!

Lives of great men all remind us
We can make our lives sublime,
And, departing, leave behind us
Footprints on the sands of time.

Footprints, that, perhaps another,
Sailing o'er life's solemn main,
A forlorn and shipwrecked brother,
Seeing, shall take heart again.

Let us, then, be up and doing,
With a heart for any fate;
Still achieving, still pursuing,
Learn to labour and to wait."

Henry Wadsworth Longfellow begins by discarding the notion that our lives are meant to be lived without purpose, that we live and die to no end or means. He declares that life is real and something to be lived with meaning and the goal of life is not the cemetery. He then makes clear that the soul, unlike the body that will return to the dust, has a purpose beyond the grave. Many of us believe that returning to dust is our destiny and after those words are spoken, life is over. However, there is much more to it than that as Wadsworth goes on to explain.

He says that temporary feelings of happiness and sadness should not lead our lives, but that we should focus on the actions that will help us to work each day so that the next will bring us closer to our purpose for living. Time is marching on and as each day passes, we are, although it is not our focus, getting closer to the grave. Time is precious and we should learn to use it wisely. As he concludes his poem, he reminds us that we should be like so many of the great ones that came before us, leaving behind footprints in the sands of time so that others might see our examples and be motivated to do the same. So let us be up and doing, with a heart that is steadfast, ready to live life full of achievement and fulfillment.

Where we are today is a plethora of acts by those who dared to go beyond their dreams. They exercised their rights and freedom to pursue a better life, greater liberty, and happiness. They, like us, wanted to leave a legacy behind. They did not want to be thieves who rob life by leaving no footprints, fingerprints, or evidence that they were ever here. They all benefited more by the journey toward their dreams than the actual achievement of their dreams.

All of us, whether we admit it or not, want to leave footprints in the sands of time so that others might say that we have traveled this way before. This is your life, no one can live it for you or take your place. On the inside of you, you have what it takes to live your life full of the purpose that was intended for you. You can face all challenges that arise by using what God has given you through your experiences. We can chose to do nothing with this knowledge and, as I say, sell our soul to the devil, or we can choose to take advantage of this knowledge and take advantage of the time we have left in life.

Selling your soul to the devil can mean taking the easiest path by compromising your beliefs. This path may seem appealing or bring happiness for the short term, but it ultimately carries long-term nega-

tive effects. I'd like to the share the origination of the expression "selling your soul to the devil," because it is relevant to our topic. It first
came about in the early 16th century. In Germany, tales sprang up
about a magician, Dr. Johannes Faust, or Fautus, who was rumored to
be in league with the devil. With his aid, Faust could supposedly perform remarkable feats. He must have traveled a great deal, as there
were reports of him from all German regions. Rumors and legends
about him began while he was still alive. He is said to have died about
1540, but the details of him have been lost.

Faust owes his first literary fame to the anonymous author of *Das
Faustbuch* (The Faust Book) published in Frankfurt am Main in 1587.
This book was a collection of tales about a number of ancient and
medieval magicians, wizards, and sorcerers who had gone by the name
of Faust. The book, attributed to the original Faust, was soon translated
and published in other countries. Das Faustbuch reveals how Faust
sought to acquire supernatural knowledge and power through a bargain
with Satan. In the pact, signed with his own blood, Faust agreed that
Mephistopheles, a devil, was to become his servant for twenty-four years.
In return, Faust would surrender himself to Satan. Mephistopheles
entertained his master with luxurious living, long intellectual conversa-
tions, and with glimpses of the spirit world. After the agreed twenty-four
years, Faust was carried off to Hell during an earthquake.

The Faust legend soon gained wide popularity and was used as a
theme by many writers. I believe that one of the most outstanding writings of the legend was formulated by Johann Wolfgang Von Goethe,
who took the story to the level of a powerful drama and introduced
the motif of a heroine, Margarete. Her abandonment by *Faust* devel-
ops some of the central themes of Goethe's Faust, a play in which
betrayal is balanced by redemption.

Johann Wolfgang Von Goethe wrote his epic *Faust: A Tragedy,* and
in Goethes's hands, the Faust story became more than a simple parable about arrogance and damnation. It became Goethe's greatest
statement to the world about the tension between soul and intellect,
humanity and divinity, good and evil, love and hate. The intention of
the original Faust books was invariably to dissuade good Christian folk
from following Faust's dark path. Since then, there have been many
stories told of the relationship of the man and the devil. Perhaps one
of the more profound and fascinating stories I have heard came from

Reverend Frederick Haynes, who told this story as heard from Dr. Jeremiah Wright.

The story is about a wonderful painting, "Checkmate," displayed in a London museum. In this painting, the devil Mephistopheles is playing a game of chess against Faust. Faust evidently has lost the game; and in this game, Faust has literally bet his soul. Mephistopheles, sitting on the other side of the chessboard, has just cried out, "Checkmate!" Because he won the game, he would collect the soul. It was all over and it was hopeless. However, one day a brilliant man was walking through the museum in with a tour group and they came to this beautiful painting entitled "Checkmate." The man stood at the foot of that painting, studying the painting. Meanwhile, the guide was telling them all about the story behind the painting, the textures on the canvas, the colors, and the semidry that were utilized in the forming of the beautiful masterpiece. Then, after telling them all about the painting, he told the tour group to come along, but this one man stayed behind, studying the painting. Finally, after some minutes had passed and the tour group had gone down the hall, they suddenly heard a loud voice crying, "It's a lie! It's a lie! The king has one more move." The brilliant man just happened to be the world chess champion and he noted that whoever had drawn the painting had mistakenly thought that Mephistopheles had really ended the game, but the king had one more move. I believe that that is the essence of this book: In this life, no matter what happens, we all have the last move with regard to our lives.

Oftentimes, when we are working to obtain our goals, circumstances, situations, and other people will say we can't do it, but in the end, the final decision to go on will be ours. We have the last move. We can get to where we want to be by working hard, maintaining our commitment, and by not always following the road of least resistance.

If we get caught up in yesterday's achievements, we will think that success will get us where we need to be. Instead, we should take courage and be encouraged from yesterday's achievements while using them to move onto the next tasks. When we learn from them and use them as stairs to get to the next level of our lives, then we will be better able to tackle today's issues and tomorrow will be much brighter. Conversely, when we linger and keep our minds on yesterday's problems, troubles, and issues, they become today's and tomorrow's problems, troubles, and issues.

Do not let life go by so that it becomes too late before you realize that you had not lived. Many people have left this life with the words of deep regret on their lips: "If only I . . ." Those are the words spoken by those that discovered later in life that they could have and should have lived a much more rewarding life rather than merely making a living. If only I would have gone to school, if only I would have not listened to those that said that I could not, if only I would have started that business, if only I would have written that book. . . . We can avoid those words of regret by living our lives now. It is up to us.

Henry David Thoreau lived for two years at Walden Pond. There, removed from everyday concerns and social pressures, he had the opportunity to discover what was important in life and he had time to write his thoughts. In "Walden" he wrote: "I went to the woods because I wished to live deliberately; to front only the essential facts of life, and see if I could not learn what it had to teach, and not, when I came to die, discover that I had not lived." He died of poor health at the age of forty-four.

It is your life, I now challenge you to go beyond your dreams and live out your purpose. As I said in the Introduction, this is a journey; we need to define a mission statement for our lives that will help guide, motivate, and inspire us to a commitment level like we have never experienced before. I hope that you will wake each day with the firm decision that your life is driven not by accident, but by purpose, and that you will look toward tomorrow with positive affirmation, not doubt or apprehension.

Now is the time to take control of your life with commitment and self-control, focusing on those things that mean the most to you and that will get you where you want and need to be. Now is the time to repeat the positive affirmation that "I can." Put aside the "How will I?""" "and hold on to "I know I can." Doing that is not as difficult as mustering up the courage to define your dreams.

This book was not intended to provide all the answers, but I pray that it helped you to open up a dialogue with yourself and helped you discover who you are and what your purpose is in life. I pray that it helped enlighten you as to what you already have on the inside of you that will make your dreams a reality. I pray that it will help you open up the world of possibilities that have inspired you to move beyond making a living and start living your life.

Today, will you dare to go beyond your dreams and realize the awesome beauty of what it is to really be you? Today, will you stand up and take on the grave responsibility for which you were created? Start now. Live your life with a sense of purpose and let it be said: **"You dared to** *Go Beyond Your Dreams* **and live the life you were intended to live."**

NOTES

NOTES

NOTES

NOTES

NOTES

NOTES

NOTES

NOTES

NOTES

NOTES

_____

_____

_____

_____

_____

_____

_____

_____

_____

_____

_____

_____

_____

_____

_____

_____

_____

_____

_____

_____

_____

NOTES

NOTES

NOTES

NOTES

NOTES